Proclamation 4

Aids for Interpreting the Lessons of the Church Year

Easter

Elizabeth Achtemeier
Paul J. Achtemeier

Series B

FORTRESS PRESS MINNEAPOLIS

PROCLAMATION 4
Aids for Interpreting the Lessons of the Church Year
Series B: Easter

Library of Congress Cataloging-in-Publication Data

(Revised for ser. B, vols. 5–8)

Proclamation 4.

Consists of 24 volumes in 3 series designated A, B, and C, which correspond to the cycles of the three year lectionary. Each series contains 8 basic volumes with the following titles: [1] Advent-Christmas, [2] Epiphany, [3] Lent, [4] Holy Week, [5] Easter, [6] Pentecost 1, [7] Pentecost 2, and [8] Pentecost 3. In addition there are four volumes on the lesser festivals.

By Christopher R. Seitz and others.

Includes bibliographies.

1. Bible—Homiletical use. 2. Bible—Liturgical lessons, English. 3. Bible—Criticism, interpretation, etc. 4. Common lectionary. 5. Church year.

I. Seitz, Christopher R. II. Title: Proclamation four.

BS534.5.P765 1991 264'.34 88-10982

ISBN 0-8006-4173-6 (series B, Easter)

The paper used in this publication meets the minimum requirements of American National Standard for Information Sciences—Permanence of Paper for Printed Library Materials, ANSI Z329.48-1984. ∞™

Manufactured in the U.S.A. AF 1-4173

95 94 93 92 91 1 2 3 4 5 6 7 8 9 10

Contents

The Resurrection of Our Lord
Easter Day 5

Easter Evening or Easter Monday 11

The Second Sunday of Easter 17

The Third Sunday of Easter 23

The Fourth Sunday of Easter 29

The Fifth Sunday of Easter 35

The Sixth Sunday of Easter 41

The Ascension of Our Lord 47

The Seventh Sunday of Easter 53

The Day of Pentecost 60

The Resurrection of Our Lord
Easter Day

Lutheran	Roman Catholic	Episcopal	Common Lectionary
Isa. 25:6-9	Acts 10:34a, 37-43	Acts 10:34-43	Acts 10:34-43 *or* Isa. 25:6-9
1 Cor. 15:19-28	Col. 3:1-4	Col. 3:1-4	1 Cor. 15:1-11 *or* Acts 10:34-43
Mark 16:1-8	John 20:1-9	Mark 16:1-8	John 20:1-18 *or* Mark 16:1-8

FIRST LESSON: ISAIAH 25:6-9
SECOND LESSON: 1 CORINTHIANS 15:1-28
GOSPEL: MARK 16:1-8

According to the author of our *Old Testament lesson,* God promised that there would come a time when death was forever done away. We do not know who recorded this promise. Most scholars agree that Isaiah 24–27 is a group of promissory eschatological oracles, stemming from various prophets belonging to the Isaiah school, that was added at a later date to the original eighth-century B.C. book of Isaiah. Along with the oracles against the foreign nations in Isaiah 13–23, it outlines the measures that God will take in his plan (cf. 25:1) to bring the universal kingdom of God on earth.

In our particular lesson, 25:6-9, several images dominate the promise. First, the coming kingdom will find its center at Mount Zion in Jerusalem (25:6). Second, Israel the people of God will experience a complete reversal of fortunes (25:8). Once they were cursed by God for their sin against him and were sent into exile and became a source of horror and hissing and cursing among the nations (cf. Jer. 29:18; 19:8; Deut. 28:37): "May you be cursed as Israel was cursed." But in God's coming kingdom, Israel will be a source of blessing in the earth (cf. Isa. 19:24-25), in fulfillment of God's promise to Abraham (Gen. 12:3).

Third, God will restore both Jews and Gentiles to fellowship with himself, a communion that is symbolized by the picture of the feast in Isa. 25:6. The nations' rebellious separation from the Lord of all will be overcome and forgiven, and they will enjoy the finest delicacies at the table of God.

Their cups will be filled with wine that has been left long on its sediment ("lees") to enhance its strength and flavor and bouquet by repeated fermentation, but then has been strained at just the right moment ("well refined"). Their bowls will be full of the choice fat part of animals that were normally reserved for the deity in the sacrificial cult. In Ps. 63:5, the latter food symbolizes the highest spiritual fellowship with God (cf. Ps. 36:8), while throughout the Scriptures, table fellowship is used as a symbol of friendship and peace (cf. Isa. 55:1-3). Thus, life in the kingdom of God is often portrayed as a banquet (Matt. 8:11; 22:2-4; Luke 14:15; Rev. 19:9), with all participants in it forgiven and joyfully, peacefully at home with their God.

Fourth, and most significant, even death will no longer disrupt human beings' fellowship with God and with one another. In the most affecting picture of all, Isa. 25:7-8 portrays the Lord lifting up the mourning veil worn by sorrowing humanity at the grave, wiping away the tears from their cheeks, and abolishing death forevermore. Such is the picture of the future that God promises humankind through his prophet.

Nothing is more crucial than the question of whether or not God fulfilled this promise spoken through Isaiah. "I delivered to you as of first importance" writes *Paul* in 1 Cor. 15:3. No day in the year bears the significance that Easter has. It is not just an appendix tacked on to the story of the cross, to be celebrated with trumpet and lilies one Sunday and then forgotten. No, Easter is the heart of the gospel, the key to Jesus' ministry (Mark 9:9), and Paul tells us clearly why. "If Christ has not been raised," he writes (1 Cor. 15:17), "your faith is futile and you are still in your sins." It is not just that Paul will be shown to have been a liar for preaching that Christ has been raised (v. 15). Rather, there is no Christian faith whatsoever without Easter—no forgiveness, no reconciliation with the Father, no eternal life, no salvation (cf. v. 2).

If the cross is all there is, then evil and sin have won the battle, and there is no victory over them. That would mean that there is no hope for this tortured planet of ours. Nothing will ever be different. There will be no day when cruelty, injustice, violence, pride, and fear are finally banished from human life. The jungle we know out there on countless city streets will just continue to exude its evil and festering poisons into the life-streams of human beings. Humanity will continue in tears and turmoil, pain and persistent wrong, until finally perhaps it blows itself up and destroys the earth in a nuclear holocaust. For if Christ is not raised from the dead, good will never triumph over human sin, and finally it is some "dark, dumb, dreaming thing that turns the handle of this evil show" (Thomas Hardy).

More than that, Paul says, if Christ has not been raised, then all those faithful souls who have believed and died in Christ have perished forever (v. 18). That would mean that there will be no one to say to a Peter or Paul, to a Dietrich Bonhoeffer or a Martin Luther King, Jr, "Well done, thou good and faithful servant. . . . Enter into the joy of your master." There will be no reward for faithful perseverance in the face of suffering and of life's outrageous fortunes, indeed, no reason to try to walk God's ways at all. As Paul puts it, "Why am I in peril every hour? . . . I die every day! What do I gain if, humanly speaking, I fought with beasts at Ephesus? If the dead are not raised, 'Let us eat and drink, for tomorrow we die' " (vv. 30-32).

In other words, if Christ has not been raised from the grave, not one of us will ever be raised to eternal life either, and that makes a mockery of trying to live the Christian life. Why bother if goodness will be overcome in the end by evil and the righteous and unrighteous share a common fate? Why "press on" if there finally is no "upward call of God in Christ Jesus" (Phil. 3:12, 14), but only the void, the darkness, the end? In that case, let's just look out for number one, and go for all the gusto we can find. The rewards of this life are to the ruthless and strong, so let's never mind on whom we trample. The only goal is to make it up that ladder of success, and never mind whose fingers on the rungs below us get bruised as we climb.

Furthermore, if Christ has not been raised from the dead, that dear face of a family member or friend whom we loved so well has been separated from us for ever, and there will be no joyful reunion at the Father's table. Love has been overcome. The good-bye has been final. And human friendship and dear, cherished bonds have no ultimate significance. Like everything else that is honorable and pure, that is lovely and gracious and excellent (Phil. 4:8), love has no lasting worth in a world where everything hastens to its doom.

Truly, if Christ has not been raised from the dead, there is no loving heavenly Father—no one to lift the veil of mourning and to wipe away the tears, no one who comes to us with a "peace" that forgives all our sins (cf. John 20:19-21). The guilty past remains a burden on our restless hearts, our human errors and wrongs are never erased, and we will die in the knowledge that we have wounded ourselves and those whom we love and have not lived our lives very well. "If Christ has not been raised, your faith is futile and you are still in your sins" (1 Cor. 15:17).

Yes, it makes all the difference as to whether or not Easter is true—as to whether or not God fulfilled that promise that he made to his people, through Isaiah.

The glad news of this Easter day, therefore, is that God kept his word. "But in fact Christ has been raised from the dead" (1 Cor. 15:20). That is not an argument in Paul's letter, not a tentative trial balloon. That is straightforward proclamation, without apology or dispute, just as the angel's statement in Mark's Gospel is also straightforward assertion: "You seek Jesus of Nazareth, who was crucified. He has risen, he is not here" (Mark 16:6). That was the apostolic, received tradition that was taught to Paul when he became a Christian (1 Cor. 15:3), that he passed on to the Corinthians (v. 1), and that now has been handed down to us on the pages of the New Testament. Jesus Christ has been raised from the dead by his Father. That is the heart of the church's gospel message. And it is "of first importance"—more significant than any other message in the world.

The *Gospel* accounts of the resurrection differ among themselves in some minor details. It is not certain which women accompanied Mary Magdalene to the tomb, or how the stone covering its entrance was removed, or whether the women were confronted by one angel or two. But there are agreements. Mary Magdalene goes to the tomb early on the first day of the week, after the Sabbath rest is past. In our Markan lesson, she is accompanied by two other women, and in the Synoptics, their purpose is to anoint Jesus' body with burial spices. All of the accounts agree that females were the first witnesses of the resurrection—a highly improbable detail if the story were made up. (On Easter, we should not try to "prove" the resurrection, but just announce it and tell what it means.) The women find the tomb empty and are told by a messenger or angels from God that Jesus is risen. The women's reaction in the Synoptics is one of fear and amazement; in Mark, they tell no one what they have experienced; in Luke, their story is not believed by the other disciples. In John, Peter too sees that the tomb is empty. In all of the Gospels, it is then the appearance of the risen Lord to the women and the disciples that convinces them of his resurrection, whether that appearance be immediately to the women themselves (Matthew), to the Magdalene (John), to the disciples in Galilee (Matthew; implied in Mark), or to the disciples gathered together in Jerusalem (Luke and John).

This received tradition of the risen Christ's appearance to Peter and the twelve apostles as a group is that which Paul has handed on to the Corinthians (1 Cor. 15:5). But, in vv. 6-7 Paul adds further appearance records, and in v. 8, he testifies that the risen Christ has appeared also to him, at his conversion (cf. 1 Cor. 9:1; Gal. 1:16; Acts 9; 22:6-16; 26:12-18). That is the event that has made Paul an apostle, even though he was "untimely born," (that is, not among the original twelve), and even though he had previously persecuted Christians. By the grace of God (v. 10), Paul was forgiven his past enmity toward the church, made a new creature in Christ (cf. 2 Cor. 5:17), and appointed an apostle to the Gentiles. He therefore can make his great statement of freedom: "By the grace of God, I am what I am." And he can testify that the working of God in him has not been in vain. God's forgiveness of Paul, and his working in him by the Spirit of the risen Christ has made Paul a new man and given him a new task and a new goal. The risen Christ can do the same for any person living in our society today.

Such is the testimony of the New Testament concerning the fulfillment of God's ancient promise, found in our Isaiah text. Paul therefore spells out the consequences of that victory in vv. 20-28. First, Christ is the "first fruits" of all those faithful who have died (v. 20). Two meanings may be involved in that statement. In Old Testament Israel, the first fruits of all products were dedicated to God, as the symbol of God's creation and ownership of all life (cf. Exod. 23:19; 34:26; Deut. 26:1-11). Christ is the "first fruits" of those who believe in him, the symbol of the fact that believers belong to God alone and that no one and no thing, not even death, can snatch them out of God's loving hand (cf. Rom. 8:38-39). Second, however, Christ's resurrection is the temporal "first fruits," the forerunner and the promise of the resurrection to eternal life of all those believers in him who come after him. Christ is the "pioneer" (cf. Heb. 12:2), the one who has gone before us into death, the one who has passed through the valley of the shadow and emerged triumphant into the new life of the kingdom. Because Christ lives now in eternity with the Father, those who trust him will also so live.

For Paul, God is working out a plan of salvation in human history that is hidden to the world and that cannot be known by the world's wisdom, but that has been revealed to Christians by the Spirit (cf. 1 Cor. 2:6-13). The plan was necessitated by the fact that like Adam, all persons have fallen under the dominion of sin and therefore are destined for death (1 Cor. 15:21-22). But the plan proceeds in human life according to a particular order, which Paul then outlines in vv. 23-28. First, Christ, the first fruits, is raised from the dead at Jerusalem and ascends into heaven, where he reigns at the right hand of God as Lord of all (cf. Rom. 8:34; Phil. 2:9-11). There follows, then, the interim time between the old age, ruled by sin, and the new age of the kingdom—the interim in which Christ and the church do battle with sin and the enemies of God. This interim time is that in which the church is now living—in which we still have to fight against the "principalities" and "powers," "against the world rulers of this present darkness, against the spiritual hosts of wickedness in the heavenly places" (Eph. 6:12). However, the outcome of the battle is sure, because Christ in his resurrection has already overcome the power of sin and death. Christ, the true Israelite, who was cursed on the cross, has become the source of blessing for the nations (cf. Isa. 25:8; Gal. 3:8-9). Therefore, when Christ comes again to set up the kingdom of God on earth, death will be done away forever, the faithful in Christ will be raised to share in Christ's eternal life and glory, and Christ will deliver to the Father a fully redeemed and transformed universe (1 Cor. 15:23-28). In that kingdom of God, become reality over all the earth, God will be "everything to every one" (v. 28), and God's plan to save his creation will have reached its final consummation.

Such is the nature of the sure hope to which the church of our day is heir, all because God has raised Jesus Christ from the dead. Sin and evil will not win the final battle. Our tortured and suffering world is not the final state of creation. The good kingdom of God comes, when all will be made whole again (cf. Rom. 8:19-23). And death is not the end for all our loved ones, for all the faithful of every nation and race, for all who have died in Christ. The void of the grave will give up its victims, the darkness of death has fled before the light of Easter morn. Jesus Christ is the first fruits, and all who trust him will be raised as he was raised, to share in the joy, the victory, the eternal life of the Father's house. God has in fact kept, and will always keep, that promise, given to us in Isaiah.

Easter Evening or Easter Monday

Lutheran	Roman Catholic	Episcopal	Common Lectionary
Dan. 12:1c-3 *or* Jon. 2:2-9	Acts 2:14, 22-32	Acts 5:29a, 30-32 *or* Dan. 12:1-3	Acts 5:29-32 *or* Dan. 12:1-3
1 Cor. 5:6-8		1 Cor. 5:6b-8 *or* Acts 5:29a, 30-32	1 Cor. 5:6-8 *or* Acts 5:29-32
Luke 24:13-49	Matt. 26:8-15	Luke 24:13-35	Luke 24:13-49

FIRST LESSON: DANIEL 12:1-3
SECOND LESSON: 1 CORINTHIANS 5:6-8
GOSPEL: LUKE 24:13-49

How does the church in our day encounter and know the risen Christ? That is really the theme of *Luke's* story of the Emmaus road and the question that he is answering for the church of his time, as well as for the church of our time. This particular material is unique to Luke's Gospel, and while portions of the account confirm other statements in the New Testament, Luke actually is addressing the later community of faith. How does the resurrection of our Lord become reality for us? That is the major concern.

Luke gives three principal answers to the question. First, with the rest of the New Testament, he affirms that we know Christ is risen, because we have the apostles' testimony to the fact. The two persons on the road to Emmaus may have been husband and wife, and the Cleopas mentioned in v. 18 may be the Clopas of John 19:25, whose wife Mary was one of the women at the foot of the cross. In their conversation with Jesus on the road, they confirm the report of the empty tomb (v. 23), of the initial skepticism of the apostles (v. 22; cf. v. 11), and of the visit of Peter and others to the tomb (cf. John 20:3-10; 1 Cor. 15:5). They themselves then are privy to the appearance of Jesus to his disciples in the room in Jerusalem (vv. 36-49), confirming the report in John 20:19-31 and 1 Cor. 15:5.

Luke 24:40 has been omitted from the RSV as an addition from John 20:27, but Luke is emphatic in his account of the appearance of the risen Lord to the disciples. Jesus has a corporeal form that is connected with his preresurrection body; he is not a spirit (v. 39), and this is emphasized by the fact that Jesus is hungry and eats the piece of broiled fish offered to him (vv. 42-43). Thus, any interpretation of the resurrection that would turn it into a merely spiritual experience, perhaps known only in the disciples' hearts, is intentionally and emphatically contradicted by Luke.

The later church can believe the testimony of the apostles concerning the resurrection. That is Luke's first point.

That is by no means sufficient for the gospel writer however, and he goes on, in the second place, to tell how the church knows the risen Lord in its present experience. We know the resurrected Christ by his presence that confronts us through the words of Scripture, Luke tells us. We have not only the apostolic testimony in the Bible that we are called on to believe. We also actually meet the living Christ through that testimony. He himself comes to us and speaks to us and enters into our lives—as real to us as if he were standing bodily before us. Three times in our passage, Luke emphasizes this fact (vv. 25-27, 32, 44-46). "Our hearts burn within us" at the presence of Christ when we understand the Scriptures; this is a persistent theme in Luke's writings (cf. Luke 16:31; Acts 2:14-36). In Luke's view, as in Matthew's and John's and Paul's, the Old Testament, in all its parts—Law, Prophets, and Writings—testify to Christ (v. 44), and the cross and the resurrection are a fulfillment of that testimony. But the words of Scripture then mediate the living Christ to us, and the church knows he is risen because it experiences his presence.

There therefore is no point in arguing with skeptics and unbelievers about the resurrection of Jesus Christ. His living person is mediated to us through the Bible, and those who do not know that Bible, cannot possibly know him alive. The church can only teach and preach its Scriptures in order to win others to faith. But similarly, church members themselves must study and know the Scriptures of both Old and New Testaments if their faith is to remain vital and the risen Christ is to accompany them along their roads in life.

Third, says Luke, we know that Christ is risen from the dead because we experience his presence among us in the sacrament of the Lord's Supper. When the risen Jesus lodges with Cleopas and Mary for the night, he, surprisingly, plays the part of host at their table (vv. 29-30). And as Jesus takes the bread and blesses it and breaks it and gives it to them, memory triggers a similar scene when Jesus fed the five thousand (Luke 9:16), and recalls to their minds the apostles' account of their final meal with their Lord (Luke 22:19). In the breaking of the bread, "their eyes were opened" and they recognized the risen Christ (vv. 31, 35).

So too the church today knows its risen Lord present at the Eucharist. The bread broken and the cup poured out trigger our memories of a final supper and of a cross suffered on our behalf. But that does not remain merely memory. Memory, in the Bible's view, always makes the past actual. The words and the actions of the Lord's Supper convey to us present reality, and Jesus eats and drinks with us as a living and "real presence" in our midst. "Where two or three are gathered in my name," he told us, "there am I in the midst of them" (Matt. 18:20). "Lo, I am with you always, to the close of the age" (Matt. 28:20), he promised. In the celebration of the Lord's Supper, the church experiences those statements to be true.

In short, the church is not a community living merely from a shared memory of a Lord who once walked among his disciples. And remembering the death and resurrection of Jesus Christ is not like remembering an event in the history of our country, such as the Declaration of Independence or the first thanksgiving. Certainly every people and every group has a story from the past that has an influence on its present shape and existence, but the fact that the church also has a shared story from the first century does not constitute the sole basis of its life. In the church's life, the past becomes present; the living Christ makes himself known through bread and wine and Scripture in each new time and place. And Christians know that Jesus Christ has been raised from the dead, because they experience his glorious, risen presence in their midst. Like Israel in the Old Testament (Exod. 33:16), their uniqueness lies in the fact that their Lord goes with them. Or as Paul would view it, the church is church because Christ is present with it in the Spirit.

For Luke, the church therefore has a response to make to such grace poured out on it. First, the church is a witness to the biblical story of what has taken place (v. 48). It is the church's responsibility to proclaim and teach to others the apostolic witness to the resurrection and the Bible's whole content, that others too may know the risen Christ.

Second, however, in the light of that testimony, the church's call is for repentance (v. 47). Because Jesus Christ has been raised from the dead and has ascended to the right hand of the Father, he has been made Lord over all, and all peoples are called to repent of their failure to acknowledge and to live in accordance with that lordship. But the church's message is not merely condemnatory of present life-styles. It is also good news, glad proclamation that in Jesus Christ all persons may be forgiven of their sinful past and present and accepted once again into the fellowship of the Father. That message of repentance and forgiveness of sins, which is repeatedly mentioned in Luke's writings (cf. Acts 2:38; 3:19; 5:31; 11:18; 17:30) is to be carried by the church to all nations, beginning back there in the first century with the apostles' first preaching in Jerusalem (v. 47), and continuing into our present day.

Luke has no illusions about the church's ability to pursue its mission of proclamation. It must be empowered by the Holy Spirit. Jesus therefore tells his disciples to wait in Jerusalem until they are clothed with power from on high (v. 49), and that empowerment will take place in the first-century church on the day of Pentecost (Acts 2). The church was granted the gift of the Spirit to enable it to carry out its God-given mission to the world (cf. John 20:21-22). Not only was the whole company of the church given the enabling Spirit, however, but according to Paul, each individual Christian, at baptism, also is given a gift of the Spirit for the building up of the church (cf. 1 Corinthians 12–14)—we all are charismatics—and we go out into the world to fulfill our discipleship, empowered not by our own feeble strengths, but by the might of the Holy Spirit of God and of his Christ.

Why is it so important that we spread the glad news of repentance and the forgiveness of sins throughout the world? If we turn now to our lesson from *Daniel,* the answer is made very clear. It is a matter of eternal life or eternal death for all persons. There comes at the end of human history, when God brings in his kingdom in its fullness, a final judgment, when the dead shall be raised, "some to everlasting life, and some to shame and everlasting contempt" (Dan. 12:2). And in New Testament terms, the judgment will be made on the basis of whether or not we have trusted in the lordship of Jesus Christ.

Daniel's is the first definite mention in the Old Testament of the resurrection of all to final judgment. Isaiah 26:19 alludes to a resurrection of the "shades," and both Job 19:25-27 and Ps. 73:24-26 hint at life after death for the faithful individual. But Daniel is moving into that apocalyptic thought-world of the intertestamental period that formed so much of the background of the New Testament.

The book of Daniel in its final form dates from 167–164 B.C. and is intended to be a reassurance to those faithful Jewish "chasidim" or saints suffering under the persecutions of the Hellenistic tyrant Antiochus IV Epiphanes (175–163 B.C.). Thus, Dan. 11:2-39 traces the course of Jewish history from the beginning of the Persian Empire (v. 2), through the reign of Alexander the Great (v. 3) and the division of his realm into four Hellenistic dynasties (v. 4). It then describes the reign of Antiochus III (vv. 10-19) and finally ends with an account of the rule of Antiochus IV Epiphanes (vv. 20-45), whose death is inaccurately depicted (vv. 40-45), a sure sign that the author lived during Epiphanes' reign. During that reign, Antiochus IV Epiphanes desecrated the temple in Jerusalem, using it for the worship of Baal Shaman and sacrificing a pig ("the abomination that makes desolate") on its altar (v. 31). The chasidim attempted to resist Antiochus IV, but were severely persecuted (v. 33), and Daniel is written to give comfort and assurance of final victory to such persecuted faithful Jews. The book therefore is very much a document of its time and cannot be used in our day to predict future events in our history.

The witness given in Daniel to the nature and working of God lends it permanent value for the church, however, and much of Daniel's theology is confirmed in the later New Testament. Thus, Matt. 25:46 and John 5:28-29 both record words of Jesus in which he speaks of the resurrection of the dead to eternal life or death, and Paul too is quite sure that we shall all finally stand before "the judgment seat of Christ" (2 Cor. 5:10). The church's message of repentance and the forgiveness of sins in Christ is therefore of urgent and ultimate importance for all persons on earth, for whether or not they trust in Christ and his gospel will determine whether they live or die eternally. There are many persons even in the church who do not believe that anymore, and the mission calling of the church has therefore lost its urgency for many of its members. But the New Testament has no doubt about it: The Christian gospel is a matter of life or death for all. Luke 24:47-49 therefore sends us out to spread that gospel.

Our epistle lesson from *1 Corinthians 5:6-8* deals with another response that the church is to make to the glad news of the resurrection—the response of godly living. Paul is dealing in this passage with immorality within the Corinthian house churches, not with those outside of the church, as vv. 9-13 clearly show. The specific example of immoral action that he mentions is that of a man living with his stepmother (v. 1), who apparently is not a Christian, since she is not criticized. Like so many in our society, the man and his friends apparently even boast about their immorality (v. 2); perhaps they see it as a sign of their "freedom," that code word used so often in our day to justify licentious practice.

Paul's argument is that such behavior is a sign, not of the new life of freedom in Christ, but of the old life of captivity to sin and death. It is the "old leaven," as Paul phrases it (vv. 6-8), drawing on the language of the Jewish Passover, in which all unleavened food was to be removed from the house before the feast was celebrated (cf. Exod. 13:7). The Passover was a celebration of God's deliverance of Israel from bondage in Egypt and from death (Exodus 12–13), and Paul draws a parallel between that deliverance and our deliverance from bondage to sin and death by Christ. Thus, he says, "Christ, our paschal lamb, has been sacrificed" (v. 7). By Christ's blood, we have been saved from bondage and the grave and delivered into the new life in the Spirit. We therefore are to walk by that Spirit of God and Christ, and not by the flesh, that is, not according to the old way of life.

Paul is quite sure that the immorality of anyone in the church will corrupt its life. Just as we say, "a bad apple spoils the whole barrel," so Paul quotes the popular proverb, "a little leaven leavens the whole lump" (v. 6): Immorality among a few church members can spread throughout the whole congregation. Paul therefore advises the Corinthians to remove (we would say "excommunicate") those practicing licentious behavior from the church and deny them entrance even to the Lord's Supper (vv. 7-11). We must remember that Paul is dealing with specific problems in the Corinthian church(es), and Matt. 18:15-20 has further canonical instructions about how to deal with immorality in the congregation. Nevertheless, Paul's pastoral instructions should be impressed on us. We can, by the manner of our life, build up or tear down the body of Christ, the church, and each one of us is responsible for the well-being in the Spirit of the whole congregation. It is a theme that Paul sounds over and over again in his letters, and he is quite sure that part of the final judgment that awaits us will deal with whether or not we have built up the life of the church (cf. 1 Cor. 3:10-17).

The church of Jesus Christ has been given marvelous gifts. It has had handed down to it the apostolic testimony to the resurrection of its Lord. It has confirmed that testimony time and again by its experience of that living Lord, who comes to it through Word and Sacrament. In response to such grace, the church is still called to proclaim its glad message of repentance and forgiveness of sins to all peoples. And it always is called to live that new life of goodness appropriate to those in Christ.

The Second Sunday of Easter

Lutheran	Roman Catholic	Episcopal	Common Lectionary
Acts 3:13-15, 17-26	Acts 4:32-35	Acts 3:12a, 13-15, 17-26	Acts 4:32-35
1 John 5:1-6	1 John 5:1-6	1 John 5:1-6	1 John 1:1—2:2
John 20:19-31	John 20:19-31	John 20:19-31	John 20:19-31

FIRST LESSON: ACTS 3:13-26
SECOND LESSON: 1 JOHN 5:1-6
GOSPEL: JOHN 20:19-31

Having discussed in our first two chapters the testimony to the resurrection of Jesus Christ in Mark, Luke, and Paul's writings, we turn now to the testimony to his postresurrection appearances given in the Gospel according to John.

According to *John,* Mary Magdalene was the first witness to the resurrection, and her presence at the empty tomb is supported by the accounts in all three of the Synoptic Gospels (Matt. 28:1; Mark 16:1; Luke 23:55; 24:1, 10). John also has Peter and the Beloved Disciple confirm that Jesus' body is gone (vv. 3-8), but Jesus' personal appearance to Mary, as she stands weeping outside of the tomb, is that which confirms her first glad discovery (vv. 11-18).

In John's theology, the accounts of the resurrection appearances are actually unnecessary to tell who Jesus is, because John considers the crucifixion to be the glorification and coronation of Christ as universal king over all, and the cross really includes Christ's resurrection and ascension to glory in its testimony (cf. 12:27-32). Nevertheless, John wants to tell how the risen Christ made himself known to the church. He therefore tells in John 20:19-29 (as in Luke 24) of Christ's appearances to the disciples in the room in Jerusalem, and the disciples are made representatives of the church as a whole.

The first appearance to ten disciples takes place on the evening of the day of resurrection, the first day of the week (v. 19). The disciples have met behind closed doors "for fear of the Jews," that is, of the Jewish authorities. Early, the New Testament church suffered persecution at the hands of the Jews for claiming that Jesus was the Messiah, and many Christians were flogged for their faith (cf. Mark. 13:9-13 and parallels). By A.D. 90, all Jewish Christians were expelled from the synagogue. Thus, the readers of John's Gospel could empathize with this portrayal of the original disciples' fear.

Unexpectedly, Christ passes through the locked doors and stands in the disciples' midst (v. 19). His resurrected body therefore is no longer bound by the limitations of the flesh, and yet it has a continuity with his earthly body—the disciples can see the marks of the nails in his hands and of the spear thrust in his side (vv. 20, 27). The only designation that we have in the New Testament for such a resurrected body comes from Paul, who terms it a "spiritual body" (1 Cor. 15:44-46), but that it has corporeal form is never doubted.

The first words that Christ says to his disciples are "Peace be with you" (vv. 19, 21). That is more than a mere greeting, however. The risen Christ is addressing Peter, who denied him, and eight men (excluding the Beloved Disciple, John 19:25-27), who deserted him at the cross. His first word to them therefore is a word of forgiveness: "Peace." He himself effects the reconciliation with them once again, as he always first forgives before he enters into fellowship with his continually sinful church.

Verse 21 forms the heart of the pericope. As God has sent the Son to reveal the Father, so the Son sends his church to witness to him throughout the world. The church is now given its mission (cf. 17:18; Matt. 28:19-20). And the purpose of the sending is made very clear: The church is to witness to Jesus Christ in order that others may believe in him through their word (cf. 17:20; 20:29) and thus have eternal life. This was the original purpose for the writing of the Fourth Gospel—that others might believe and thus have life (20:31)—and so too it is the purpose for which the church is sent out.

The importance of this mission is emphasized, then, by v. 23. If the church witnesses to Jesus Christ, those who come to believe because of that witness will receive forgiveness. But if the church does not carry out such a mission, others will be lost. On the testimony of the church to Jesus Christ hangs the eternal life or death of others (cf. Matt. 16:19; 18:18).

In v. 22, therefore, the disciples (representing the church) are equipped for their mission by the gift of the Holy Spirit. The church does not testify to its Lord by its own power, but by the Spirit of God and Christ lent to it. The verse is intended to be the equivalent of the account of Pentecost given in Acts 2. As in that latter passage, v. 22 here in John signals a radical newness broken into human history. The verse reminds one of the account in Gen. 2:7, in which the Lord breathes the breath of life into Adam and he becomes a living being. The risen Christ here breathes the Holy Spirit into the disciples to make a new creation. The new age has begun. The old age must now give way to the powers of eternal life in Christ, and it is those powers that the church will mediate to others when it testifies to Jesus Christ (cf. 7:38-39).

The Fourth Gospel has a very pronounced doctrine of the Holy Spirit, and the full gifts of that Spirit are here conveyed to the disciples. First, the Holy Spirit is given to the disciples or the church as the risen Christ's continuing presence with them (14:18-19). No longer is our Lord bound by the limitations of time and space. Now because he is risen from the dead, his Spirit is given to the church in whatever place. Thus, he can tell his disciples that it is to their advantage that he go away, that is, that he be crucified and exalted on the cross (16:7). After the cross and resurrection, he returns to his church in the Spirit (14:25-26; 16:13-14) and dwells in it (14:17). The Spirit of Christ then witnesses to him (15:26), recalls to mind all that he has done, teaches the church the full truth about him, and enables the church to live in love within its own fellowship (14:18-21). Furthermore, it is through the working of the Spirit of Christ, mediated by the church to others, that they are convicted of sin and righteousness and judgment (16:8-11); the Spirit continues the work of the Son and of the Father in the world.

There follows in vv. 24-29 the story of the disciple who has acquired the unfortunate title of "doubting Thomas." The popular title is unfair to this disciple who was absent at the time of Jesus' first appearance, because Thomas really asks no more than the other ten disciples had already received—the sight of Jesus' wounded hands and side (vv. 25, 20); he simply wants to be included among the recipients of the revelation. When Thomas is told that he may be included, there is no mention of his insistence on seeing the wounds. Instead, his response of faith goes far beyond that of the other ten disciples. They were simply "glad when they saw the Lord" (v. 20). Thomas bursts out in the ultimate confession, "My Lord and my God!" (v. 28). The text does not say that Thomas fell at Christ's feet, but it is hard to imagine that he did not; when one meets the Lord, one bows down in adoration.

The point of the Thomas story, however, is stated in v. 29, and it is meant to reinforce the message of vv. 21 and 23. Those persons will be blessed who, though not having seen the risen Lord with their own eyes, yet believe in him through the church's apostolic witness to him. The church is sent out to proclaim that Jesus is the Christ, the Son of God, in order that all persons may believe and have life in his name (v. 31). Thus, such persons will be blessed if they believe that message of the church (v. 29), because they will indeed have eternal life in Christ (cf. 11:25-27).

Through faith comes blessed and abundant eternal life (cf. 10:10), and through the apostolic witness of the church comes faith; that is really the major meaning of this passage.

Our other two stated texts may be viewed as supplements to that message of John's. *Acts 3:13-26* portrays the preaching of the early church, represented by Peter, and the main purpose of the passage is to give the church's witness to who Jesus Christ is. This is Peter's second long address in Acts, and it is occasioned by the healing of the forty-year-old man (4:22) who was lame from birth (3:2) and who begged at the Beautiful Gate of the temple in Jerusalem. Those persons who witnessed the healing were astounded by it (3:10), and they have come together in Solomon's portico (v. 11)—that porch which faced the Mount of Olives on the Eastern side of the temple and that was built by Herod the Great (37 B.C–A.D. 4) during his temple restorations.

In his address, Peter makes it very clear that Jesus Christ is not some mysterious figure suddenly dropped from the blue. No, he is the completion and the final interpretation of the two thousand years of Old Testament history that have preceded him, and he really can be understood only in such terms. His death on the cross was foretold by the prophets (v. 18), just as his coming again is also foretold (v. 21).

As the fulfillment of Old Testament sacred history, Christ has gathered up in his person three major promises in the Old Testament. First, our Lord is the fulfillment of the promise to Abraham that through his descendants, all the families of the earth would be blessed (v. 25; Gen. 12:3). And Peter, speaking here to Jews, tells them that Christ has been sent to them first, to bring the blessing of God upon them first of all (v. 26). They have crucified that one who was literally God-in-human-flesh on earth: the "Holy and Righteous One," the "Author of Life"—those titles can only be used of God (vv. 14-15). Nevertheless, God will blot out their sins against him if they repent and turn from their unbelief. They will be reconciled once again to their Lord, in whose presence they will find "times of refreshing"—a lovely description of the believer's life with the Lord (v. 19). The Christ of God can only be received by faith (cf. Luke 3:8-9). Being a Jew—or being a church member—does not automatically include one in Christ's company. God's promised blessing on all the families of the earth may be had only through trust in Jesus Christ.

Second, Peter's speech testifies that Jesus Christ was the fulfillment of God's promise of a Suffering Servant, who would give his life as a ransom for many and by whose stripes all the nations would be healed and counted righteous in God's sight (vv. 13, 26; Isa. 52:13—53:12). God's offer of forgiveness in this speech of Peter's is based on that ransoming, healing death of Christ. No one can erase our sins against God's love and lordship except God himself through his Suffering Servant.

Third and apparently closely connected with the figure of the Suffering Servant (cf. Deut. 34:5; 3:24), Jesus Christ is, according to Peter, the fulfillment of the promise of a "prophet like Moses" (vv. 22-24; Deut. 18:15-16). In his sermon in Deuteronomy, Moses promised the Israelites that God would raise up for them a prophet like himself, to whom they should listen in obedience. The Old Testament itself probably considered that all of the prophets fulfilled this promise, each in his turn—certainly Jeremiah is understood as this Mosaic prophet. But by the time of the New Testament there had arisen the eschatological expectation of a special prophet, sent from God, who would fulfill the Mosaic role (cf. 7:37; John 1:21, 25; 6:14; 7:40). He would mediate God's word to human beings and he would intercede and suffer for the sins of his people, as Moses has done (cf. Deuteronomy 9; 1:37; 4:1). Jesus Christ is now this eschatological prophet, proclaims Peter, and it is to him that obedience is owed in all things. Indeed, if the word of such a prophet is not heeded, one cannot be a member of God's people (v. 23)—a sobering fact to keep before the church in our day, when so many think that God just overlooks all sin.

This speech of Peter's ties the two testaments firmly together. It enlarges our understanding of who Jesus Christ is. And it holds out once again before the church, which is the new Israel in Christ, the gracious offer of the forgiveness of all our sins, if we will repent and believe.

Finally, our lesson in *1 John* adds one more dimension to our understanding of what it means to have faith in Jesus Christ. First John was written to deal with the problem of divisions in the church. Apparently a theological dispute over Christology and its implications had arisen, and a dissident group "went out" from the congregation (1 John 2:19). They had done so because they had misunderstood the Christology of the Fourth Gospel.

In that Gospel, there is very little said about Jesus' humanity, but a great deal said about his divinity, because the Fourth Gospel was directed to Jewish Christians, and no Jew had to be convinced that Jesus was human; it was Jesus' divinity that the Jews disputed. The group in 1 John that had left the church therefore denied Jesus' real incarnation (4:2); they celebrated baptism but not the Lord's Supper, which commemorated Jesus' death (5:6); they believed themselves to be sinless and living in the Spirit (1:5-10); and they neglected ethical action and love within the body of Christ (3:11-18). They split the church, and for the writer of 1 John that is a mortal sin, which is unforgivable (5:16).

True faith, for the author of 1 John, has two characteristics. First, it confesses that Jesus—born in the flesh, born of woman, crucified on the cross as an expiation for our sins and for the sins of the world (2:2), risen again—is the Christ, the Son of God (5:1, 5). Second, however, it manifests itself in loving action toward those in the church of Jesus Christ. "Everyone who loves the parent loves the child" reads our text (5:1), and "child" probably refers to those other believers who are mentioned also in 4:20. Apart from love for one's fellow church members, one cannot say that one loves God or Jesus Christ, for the Father and the Son have commanded that we love one another as they have loved us (cf. John 13:34-35; 15:9-12). To love God means to keep his commandments (John 14:15), and his commandment is that we love one another.

Both of these emphases were present in the Gospel according to John, and the writer of 1 John (whose identity we do not know and who cannot be identified with the author of the Gospel) is giving an accurate reading of the Fourth Gospel over against the claims of the dissidents who have left the congregation. Such is true faith, says the author—faith that believes the whole story, human and divine, about Jesus Christ, and faith that obeys the commandment to love within the church. Such faith, the author is quite sure, can overcome the world (5:4). No obstacle and no opposition will prevent its victory.

We usually read 1 John in general terms, but its concern for the unity of the church needs to be emphasized. Splitting churches is sinful. By the Spirit of Christ given us, therefore let us love one another.

The Third Sunday of Easter

Lutheran	Roman Catholic	Episcopal	Common Lectionary
Acts 4:8-12	Acts 3:13-15, 17-19	Acts 4:5-12	Acts 3:12-19
1 John 1:1—2:2	1 John 2:1-5a	1 John 1:1—2:2	1 John 3:1-7
Luke 24:36-49	Luke 24:35-48	Luke 24:36b-48	Luke 24:35-48

FIRST LESSON: ACTS 4:5-12
SECOND LESSON: 1 JOHN 1:1—2:2
GOSPEL: LUKE 24:36-49

(For a discussion of the general themes of 1 John and of the setting of Acts 3:13—4:12, see the previous chapter. For a treatment of the total message of Luke 24:13-49, see the chapter for Easter Evening/Easter Monday).

God is working to overcome the evil effects of the sins of the world. That is the thrust of these three stated lessons and the theme that ties them together. Suppose we enter our discussion at *Luke* 24:44, where Jesus Christ is understood as the fulfillment of the entire history of Israel in the Old Testament. There are not many modern churchgoers who understand how that is so, but such knowledge is basic to an appropriation of the Christian faith. It therefore is sometimes wise for preachers briefly to review the history given us in the Bible.

The Old Testament tells us that in the beginning, God created the world "very good," but that our rebellion against God—our attempts to run our own lives and to be our own gods and goddesses—corrupted God's good creation. By such sin, we broke our intimate relation with our Creator, disrupted every form of human community, distorted God's good gifts of work and marriage and family, despoiled the beauty of the earth, and brought on ourselves God's curse, with its inevitable sentence of death.

In answer to that sinful rebellion, the God of love therefore called Abraham and Sarah out of Mesopotamia to be the forebears of a new community. To them he promised the restoration of the relationship with himself, in a covenant; the benefits of a new community that knew how to live in justice and righteousness under his guiding law and lordship; a new life in a new land, flowing with milk and honey, where there would be "rest" from all enemies; and blessing brought upon all the families of the earth through their descendants.

God worked in Israel through the years, gradually fulfilling each of these promises. When he had entered into covenant with Israel at Mount Sinai, and made them a new people, and given them guiding commandments, and brought them to the land promised to them, he even added a new promise. He swore to Israel that there would never be lacking a Davidic king to sit on their throne, and as long as that king reigned in righteousness and justice, Israel would live in his favor. Moreover, as we read in the prophets, it was God's hope to draw all nations into the community of Israel, that all people might become the recipients of his blessings to his chosen people. In other words, despite human sin, God set out in Israel to make his creation "very good" once again.

But Israel, like us, would have none of it. She wanted, as we want, to run her own life and to determine her own future. Repeatedly rebelling against her Lord, she was just as repeatedly forgiven and called to repentance and shown the way to walk in her communal and individual life. Finally, however, the Lord was forced to send her into exile for her rebellion against his rule. Yet the prophets were sure that God would nevertheless keep his promises to his people and make them a source of blessing for all the families of the earth.

The New Testament, then, confirms that God kept his word. In Jesus Christ, "the son of Abraham, the son of David" (Matt. 1:1), God once again made a people for himself, restoring their relationship to him through a "new covenant" given at the last supper in that upper room; forming them into a new universal community called the Christian church, with Jesus Christ as the chosen cornerstone; giving them new commandments by which to walk in their daily lives; setting them on a pilgrimage toward a promised place of "rest" in Christ; overcoming the sentence of death for sin through the crucifixion and resurrection; setting over them as their Lord the new David, born in Bethlehem; and calling them to proclaim the glad message that in that Christ, all the families of the earth could find blessing.

In that one history, told to us in the Bible, God began to overcome the effects of our sinful rebellion against him, and to set up his kingdom on earth, through Jesus Christ. That is the history in which the Christian church now lives, and because that history has taken place, our Lord can say, in Luke 24:44, that the entire Old Testament witnesses to him. The mission of the church, then, is to tell that history to all peoples, so that all may believe it and enter into it and be restored to relationship with their God. By trust in our Lord Jesus Christ, who is God's fulfillment of all his promises, all persons are offered the forgiveness of sins mentioned in Luke 24:47, or the expiation of which we are told in 1 John 2:2, or the salvation proclaimed in Acts 4:12. And this one story of God's work to save his creation is that to which our Lord refers in Luke 24:44-45.

First John 1:1-4, then, is offering its own comment on that history of salvation. First, the author attests to the truth of the account. Eternal life was made manifest through Jesus Christ (v. 2), and the author maintains that the apostles saw and heard and touched the Lord. They thus are proclaiming what they themselves have experienced (vv. 1, 3). Second, through the revelation given in Jesus Christ, they have been restored to fellowship with God and with his Son (v. 3), which is the definition of salvation unto eternal life. They therefore are writing the letter in order that its recipients, too, may enter into that saving fellowship and thus experience the joy that they already know (v. 4; the verse should probably read, "that *your* joy may be complete).

The main concern of the author of 1 John, however, is with those who claim that they have no sin and that they therefore are already spiritual beings, experiencing the salvation of God. As we said in chapter three, 1 John is dealing with a dissident group that has denied the real humanity of Jesus and his death on the cross for sin. That dissident group has split the church and left the fellowship of the congregation (2:4). The author's concern about them is evident in the "if" phrases in 1:5—2:1: "If we say we have no sin," "if we confess our sins," "if we say we have not sinned," "if anyone does sin." It is with sin that the author is primarily concerned and obviously he thinks we all are sinners in constant need of the expiation or "covering over" of sin afforded us by the cross of Christ.

That is not a view that is shared by large segments of our society. "Sin" has become an almost unused term these days, because many persons think they do not sin. It is not that they consider themselves already saved, as the opponents in 1 John did (although there are a few who hold such views in our time). Rather, many persons no longer believe that they are responsible to God, and where there is no responsibility, there is nothing that is called sin. Instead, such persons will attribute evil acts to psychological illness ("he must be sick"), or to natural human error ("I goofed"; "That's human nature"), or sociological and familial influences ("I live in an evil environment"; "my parents didn't raise me right"). The cure for human wrongdoing, therefore, is thought to lie in therapy, or in education, or in changing the environment, or perhaps these days even in engineering the genetic code. God is totally absent from the picture, human responsibility to him is never considered, and human beings will, by their own cleverness, eliminate evil from the world.

When I was preaching in the church of one of our large universities, I was told before the service that the congregation no longer liked the original wording of the General Confession: "We have done what we ought not to have done, and there is no health in us." There is lots of health in us, that congregation maintained. There is no such thing as original sin or total depravity, in which our entire being is considered to be touched and distorted by the power of sin. We can save ourselves, was the view, by the goodness and power that are inherent in us. As one feminist writer has put it, "All we need is love."

Over against such self-deception, 1 John gives several arguments. First, to claim that we have no sin and yet to destroy the bonds between human beings, as we all do, is to lie and to walk in darkness. God is light, and those who walk in his light maintain the ties of human love and fellowship (1:6-7). Second, if we say we have not sinned, we make God a liar, because God has offered Jesus Christ on the cross, to atone for our sins and for the sins of the whole world (1:10; 2:2). Third, however—and this is the good news—if we will confess our sins, God will forgive them. Not only has Christ offered the expiation for our sins on the cross (2:2), but he is also a righteous advocate for us before the Father, pleading our case and interceding for us (2:1). And because of that advocacy, God will not only forgive us our evil past, but also cleanse us and make us whole, sanctifying us in our present and future lives (1:9). It is only when we know we are forgiven that we can confess that we are sinful, for then we know that we will not be eternally lost because of our sins. The grace of God makes repentance possible, and that grace is offered us in Jesus Christ.

Such saving grace is offered also through our Scripture lesson in Acts. *Acts 4:5-12* continues the story that began in 3:1. In the name of Christ, Peter has healed the lame man at the Beautiful Gate of the temple, and he has explained in his speech in 3:12-26 who Jesus Christ is. As a result of Peter's speech and the preaching of the resurrection by both Peter and John, some five thousand persons have been converted to faith in the Lord (4:4).

This is annoying to the Sadducees, who do not believe in any resurrection of the dead (cf. Mark 12:18; Acts 23:8), but it is also alarming to the Jewish authorities in Jerusalem, who make up the Sanhedrin or ruling council of the Jews. Among their number are Annas, who was high priest from A.D. 6–15; Joseph Caiaphas, his son-in-law, who served as high priest at the time of Jesus' trial (cf. Matt. 26:3, 57; John 18:13-14, 24); a levitical "captain of the temple," whose office had arrested Jesus (Luke 22:4, 52); and other members of the high priestly family, as well as elders and scribes (Acts 4:5-6). Little wonder that such a group is disturbed by the preaching of the apostles! They are indeed the "builders" who rejected God's chosen "stone" (4:11). But now God is rejecting them and erecting his own edifice of the church, with Jesus Christ as the chief cornerstone: God's building versus human works; God's authority versus petty man's. It is always so in the power plays that characterize the history of salvation in this world.

Peter and John are therefore arrested and held in custody for a night and then brought before the Jewish leaders (4:3, 7). Such an arrest was not illegal, because the Jewish Sanhedrin did have the authority to sit as a judicial court, and to guard Jewish life, custom, and law.

Peter's defense before the authorities is inspired in him by the Holy Spirit, but it is remarkably benign, perhaps because it is clear that the authorities really have no case against him and John. The two apostles have merely done a good deed for a person with a disability and that surely is no crime (4:9). Indeed, the only action the Sanhedrin can take is to admonish the two disciples not to speak or teach further in the name of Jesus (4:18). Were the Sanhedrin to do otherwise, they would violate their own law and suffer the indignation of the crowd that has witnessed the remarkable healing of the lame man (vv. 16, 21). In response to such admonition, Peter and John reply that they cannot but speak of what they have seen and heard, and that they must obey not the commands of men, but of God (vv. 19-20): God's action versus that of human beings, God's authority above that of man's.

Further, despite the assured outcome of the case, Peter uses it as an opportunity to witness, using a quotation from Ps. 118:22: The lame man has been healed by the power of Jesus Christ, who was crucified, was raised from the dead, and who has become the cornerstone of God's new people (vv. 10-11). And then Peter utters that confession that has formed the heart of the church's gospel ever since: "And there is salvation in no one else, for there is no other name under heaven given among men by which we must be saved" (v. 12). The church's message is that our salvation from God is given us solely through Jesus Christ. Such a message claims for the gospel of the New Testament a uniqueness over against every other religion of the world, and such a gospel claims for Jesus Christ the sole title of Lord of all, over against the testimonies given for every other religious figure. Every other pathway to God is ruled out; all other religions are made secondary. No one comes to the Father but by Christ (cf. John 14:6), and no one else can give salvation. In our pluralistic and polytheistic world, that is an audacious claim.

Sometimes, of course, such a claim seems offensive to many persons, and they will raise the arguments about all the harm Christianity has done in the world by claiming to be unique—persecuting the Jews, mounting the crusades, winning converts by torture in the Inquisition. To be sure, the Christian faith cannot be spread by coercion and imposition. It cannot even be spread by arguments over its uniqueness. Rather, other persons will be drawn into the church solely by the means that Peter and John used in our Scripture lesson—by testimony on the part of believers to what they have seen and heard of their Lord. Others will come into the community of believers when they hear the "old, old story"—that story that we told in our discussion of our passage from Luke, that story that has become our own personal story of salvation in our Lord, that story of the new life we have received from him.

In using Acts 4:12 for the text of a sermon, therefore, perhaps the best attitude is to preach it, not as a claim but as the gracious invitation of God to a world weary with its sin. Many persons will deny that there is such a thing as sin and that they have any responsibility toward their God. And yet, our God has made our hearts restless until they rest in him. Every person sometimes yearns for some surcease from the guilt in his or her heart, for some rest from the fear of death, for some relief from the evil that corrupts the world all around, for some assurance that human life is not a meaningless evil joke, perpetrated by chance. Here then, in Acts 4:12, is the satisfaction of all those yearnings. In Jesus Christ, God has graciously forgiven us all our sin and wrong. He has made us participants in his good purpose and assured us of eternal life. And he has given us that joyous faith that overcomes the world. Surely, no more gracious gifts have ever been offered to humankind. Thanks be to God that there is the name Jesus Christ given under heaven, by which we may be saved!

The Fourth Sunday of Easter

Lutheran	Roman Catholic	Episcopal	Common Lectionary
Acts 4:23-33	Acts 4:8-12	Acts 4:32-37	Acts 4:8-12
1 John 3:1-2	1 John 3:1-2	1 John 3:1-8	1 John 3:18-24
John 10:11-18	John 10:11-18	John 10:11-16	John 10:11-18

FIRST LESSON: ACTS 4:23-33
SECOND LESSON: 1 JOHN 3:1-2
GOSPEL: JOHN 10:11-18

There are key biblical motifs in these three lessons that either bind them together with one another or with the Bible as a whole. All of them are extremely important.

Most prominent, of course, is that of the good shepherd in our Gospel lesson. John 10:1-18 has two figures for Jesus, one as the door of the sheep, and the other as the good shepherd, and it is with the latter that our lesson is concerned. Jesus calls himself the "good shepherd," and this is the only passage in the Bible in which that combination of words is found. He is termed the "great shepherd" in Heb. 13:20, the "chief Shepherd" in 1 Pet. 5:4, the "Shepherd and Guardian of your souls" in 1 Pet. 2:25. In Rev. 7:17 he is both the Lamb and the shepherd who will guide the faithful martyred to the waters of eternal life, and of course, Jesus himself used the figure of a shepherd in a parable (Luke 15:4-7).

Jesus' use of the figure for himself probably depends on its use in the Old Testament. All are familiar with the figure in Psalm 23 and in Isa. 40:11, but Jesus probably takes it from Ezek. 34:11-16, 23-24. God promises that, in the eschatological age, he will set over his people his shepherd David. In short, the term is a royal figure (as it is also in Isa. 40:11), consonant with the emphasis on Jesus' kingship in the Gospel according to John (see John 19), and the connection with the office of the Davidic king or Messiah shows that the title must not be sentimentalized.

Jesus is the "good" shepherd because he lays down his life for his sheep. That emphasis is repeated four times in our passage (vv. 11, 15, 17, 18) and it forms the major theme of the text. Unlike the false shepherds of Ezek. 34:1-6, who have used the sheep for their own advantage (v. 3) and let them be scattered to become prey to beasts (vv. 5-6), who have not strengthened the weak, or healed the sick, sought the lost or ministered to the crippled (v. 4), Jesus is the shepherd who cares so much for the sheep that he will even die for them to protect them from harm (cf. John 15:13; 1 John 3:16). He loves and knows his own flock intimately—as intimately as the Father and Son know and love one another—and his flock loves and knows him (John 10:14). Therefore nothing, not even death, will separate those who love and know Jesus from his shepherding care.

It is really this willingness of our Lord to lay down his life for his followers that distinguishes him from all other shepherds. It is not because that self-sacrifice is so unusual—many persons have given their lives for others—but because the death of Jesus alone rescues his sheep from death. Lots of so-called leaders tell us what to do about our death. Just face death bravely, say some existentialists; forget about personal immortality, writes a leading feminist; prepare to spin out never-ending good and bad reincarnations on your wheel of karma, proclaim the New Age religionists. But the good shepherd, the appointed Messiah of God, alone can deal with the death of us all. He does so by laying down his life for us and rising again, and by that act, Jesus Christ, and he alone, can end the reign of death forever (John 11:25-26).

The second major motif, found in all three of our lessons, is that of the plan of God. Jesus' crucifixion is not merely the result of his will—although John emphasizes that Jesus goes freely to the cross—but it is also part of God's plan, in order to give eternal life to the world. "This charge I have received from my Father," Jesus says (10:18). Similarly, in Acts 4:27-28, the death of Jesus at the hands of Herod and Pilate, and of the Jews and Gentiles, is that which God has "predestined to take place." God has used the wrath and opposition of men and women against his Son to praise and serve his loving purpose for his world.

This plan or purpose of God, however, is by no means limited to those few years of the ministry of Jesus of Nazareth. In our Acts lesson, we four times find the word "servant(s)" (vv. 25, 27, 29, 30). The disciples' prayer acknowledges that from the time of David in 1000 B.C. up until their present time (ca. A.D. 100), the actors in the holy history have been the servants of God, carrying out that which God has purposed in his plan of salvation: God's plan has spanned the centuries. Then, in 1 John 3:2, the vision is extended even further, to the end of time. God has made Christians his children and has an even greater future planned for them in his eternal kingdom. God's purpose encompasses human history and is being worked out in his good time. He is in charge of the course of our lives and will bring them to his goal for them.

Third in this discussion of major motifs is that of the power of God. There is no doubt that God has the power to accomplish his plan for the world. There is great emphasis in the Fourth Gospel on the love of God, but there is also repeated emphasis on the power of God, without which his love would be ineffectual. Jesus, acting on behalf of God, is totally in charge of what human beings do to him. "No one takes my life from me," he says (v. 18); he is master in the course of events (cf. 14:31). Thus, no one can take him by force against his will (6:15; 2:24); Caiaphas must unknowingly serve his purpose (11:49-52), and Pilate must acknowledge Jesus' kingship on the cross (19:22).

So, too, in our Acts lesson, the power of God is made manifest. Over against the threats against the disciples' lives, they pray for boldness to speak (v. 29; cf. 4:13; 14:3) and to testify to the resurrection of Christ (v. 33; cf. 1:22). Noteworthy is the fact that they do not pray for protection or for vengeance on their enemies or for release from their ministry. No, absolutely convinced of the resurrection of their Lord, they pray only for boldness in testifying to it. And that power is granted by the gift of the Holy Spirit (cf. 2:4), which shakes the very room they occupy and fills them all with courage (v. 31), so that they are able to testify with "great power" (cf. 1:8) and to spread the gospel throughout the Mediterranean world. God has the power to carry out his plan of salvation for his world, and through his Son and his Spirit, he lends that power to his faithful servants.

Not only is power given to speak and to testify to the resurrection, however, but power is also given the disciples to heal, as Peter and John healed the lame man at the Beautiful Gate of the temple. (Our passage follows immediately on that episode and its consequences; see the two preceding discussions). And power is given to the disciples to perform "signs and wonders" in the name of Jesus (v. 30; cf. 2:43; 14:3). The God who so loved the world that he gave his only begotten Son, is the God of unconquerable, inexhaustable, never-ceasing power.

Fourth, common to all three of our lessons is the thought that such power of God also creates community. We might say that by his work God draws believers into his united family, for both the Fourth Gospel and 1 John emphasize the fact that through faith we become "children of God" (John 1:12-13; 1 John 3:2, 10); indeed, such a fact is the dominating motif of chapter five in 1 John.

The understanding of the faithful as God's children has a long history in the Bible. In the Old Testament, Israel is adopted as God's "son" at the time of the exodus (Exod. 4:22-23; Hos. 11:1; Jer. 3:4, 19; 31:20; Isa. 1:2), and it is this adoption that Paul compares to our adoption as "sons" or children of God, in Gal. 4:4-7 (cf. 3:26). Thus, in the Bible, the fact that we are children of God is not based on the thought of God's creation of us, but on his act of redeeming us, which we appropriate by faith. The faithful—all who receive Jesus Christ and believe on his name—are given "power to become children of God" by the work of the Holy Spirit (John 1:12-13), and that Spirit is all that enables them to call God "Abba, Father" (Gal. 4:6; Rom. 8:14-17). Thus God, working in us by the power of his Holy Spirit, takes us into his household and makes us his children.

There is no doubt, then, that such a "family" or community, created by the power of God, is a united community. Our lesson from Acts tells us that "the company of those who believed were of one heart and soul" (4:32), so much so, that all spirit of competition and selfishness was eliminated from their midst, although the following story of Ananias and Sapphira, in Acts 5: 1-11, shows that some were still subject to the grasping spirit of this world. But most of the disciples, says Acts, "had everything in common" (v. 32), so that all contributed their goods to the common need and there was "not a needy person among them" (vv. 34-35).

Some interpreters have used these verses in Acts 4 and 5 to argue for communism or socialism in our present political system. But Acts is not dealing with political structures, and there is no way these verses can be ripped from their historical context and applied in general fashion to modern pluralistic nations. Luke, the writer of Acts, is dealing here with the community of faith, and within that community, he tells us, no person is in need. The spirit of selfishness, of greed, of competition with one's neighbors is gone. No faithful disciple tries to "keep up with the Joneses," to outdo them in conspicuous consumption, or to relegate them to a lesser status on the basis of material wealth. Economic classes must not exist in the Christian church; no trustees or other wealthy persons are to be especially honored for their riches or even for their largesse toward the church. All are of "one heart and soul," equally valued and honored in the community. And so, too, material need must not exist in the Christian church. No one should be in want, as 1 John also emphasizes (3:16-17). The church extends its generosity to every needy member, and everyone shares equally in the welfare of all. These verses stand in judgment against the class distinctions and self-seeking often found in our modern church, and they remind us that liberality toward all is the result that follows when we receive the Holy Spirit.

The community or household that God's power, which is given by the Holy Spirit, creates is also a community of prayer, as our Acts lesson illustrates. Acts tells us elsewhere that the New Testament church was bound together from the first in common prayer to the Father (1:14) and that they devoted themselves to the apostles' teaching, to "fellowship, to the breaking of bread [evidently a reference to the Lord's Supper], and the prayers" (2:42), as well as to the "ministry of the word" (6:4). This was a community that looked to God for its life and sustenance, in the face of all opposition to its mission, and of course there is no other source who can create and sustain the Christian church. By his Spirit, God created the church (cf. Acts 2) and by the same power he sustains and guides its life. The church therefore is that community that turns always to him in its devotion.

The power of God, working through his Holy Spirit, also purifies the church in righteousness, however. To live in God's community is to do right. God is righteous and so the believer too must be righteous (1 John 2:29). Certainly 1 John's definition of righteousness has to do primarily with love of one's fellow church members, and the unrighteous in 1 John's thought are primarily those who have split the church and gone out from the congregation (see the preceding discussions). But there is also the amazing thought in 1 John, as in Paul's letters (cf. 2 Cor. 3:18), that God is at work in the lives of church members to recreate them in his image (1 John 3:2). Believers are already God's children, but God continues to work in their lives. And when the kingdom comes, they will see God as he is, and they will find themselves to be like God, purified by his Spirit (1 John 3:3), so that they reflect his image of purity. In other words, the power of God at work in us is sanctifying us, so that, at the end, we will be that true image of God that we were intended in the beginning to be (cf. Gen. 1:26-28).

Church members must strive to participate in that work of sanctification, however. Each one is to "purify himself" (1 John 3:3); that is, each one is to strive to do the right, to love his or her fellow church members, and to walk according to God's commandments. In the Johannine literature, the principal commandment is "to love one another" as Jesus has loved us (cf. John 15:12), to sacrifice ourselves for one another as he has sacrificed himself for us (John 15:13). God's power works that ability in us, but we are to cooperate with that power and not to hinder it. As Paul would put it, we are to work out our own salvation with fear and trembling, for God is at work in us, both to will and to work for his good pleasure (Phil. 2:13).

Finally, the power of God at work in the Christian "family" also creates a community that does not take to itself undue pride and self-righteousness. In one sense, 1 John exhibits a spirit of partisanship that is much too harsh. Its writer calls those who have gone out from the congregation "antichrists"

(2:18), and he is sure that they have committed the unpardonable sin (5:16). Such language is a sure mark of controversy, and often such language is much too heavy in its absolutism over against the opponents whom it condemns. That is one of the reasons why it is so marvelous that we have the whole canon given to us. The Scriptures interpret and balance one another, and set each book of the canon in its proper perspective.

Certainly that is what our lesson from the Fourth Gospel does for these views in 1 John. Over against all of our proud tendencies to cut ourselves off as Christians from the rest of the world and to claim that we alone are the favored of God, our Lord speaks his words in John 10:16: "I have other sheep, that are not of this fold; I must bring them also, and they will heed my voice." Unknown to us in the Christian church, there are others outside of our "family" whom Jesus knows and loves, and they too will be brought into God's household and given a portion in his kingdom. Our pride and self-righteousness are tempered by the love of God in his Son, who gave his life for the whole wide world, not just for us. And God, by his power, will save a multitude far beyond our imagining and sinful calculations.

Thus, our Lord holds out to us the final vision of the kingdom of God come on earth. "There shall be one flock, one shepherd," he says (v. 16). God finally will be confessed as Lord by all (cf. Phil. 2:10-11), and over all God will set his one good shepherd, Jesus Christ, to love and care for his sheep.

The Fifth Sunday of Easter

Lutheran	Roman Catholic	Episcopal	Common Lectionary
Acts 8:26-40	Acts 9:26-31	Acts 8:26-40	Acts 8:26-40
1 John 3:18-24	1 John 3:18-24	1 John 3:18-24	1 John 4:7-12
John 15:1-8	John 15:1-8	John 14:15-21	John 15:1-8

The element that unifies these three texts is the power and activity of the Spirit of God. The Spirit represents the same power of God by which Jesus overcame death, and that empowers the mission of the Church. It is thus appropriate that it be emphasized in this time between Easter and Pentecost. It is a time of remembering the Spirit's power in Jesus' resurrection and anticipating its coming power in the mighty events of Pentecost. These Sundays, poised between remembrance and expectation, thus mirror accurately the situation of the church, poised as it is between the appearance and return of Christ.

FIRST LESSON: ACTS 8:26-40

This passage continues the progress of Christian witness announced in Acts 1:8: Judea, Samaria, and the whole world. With this passage, the witness stretches beyond Palestine and indeed moves to a new continent, Africa. Interestingly enough, Philip is again the instrument of this new move, as he had been in the move into Samaria (Acts 8:6-7). He is therefore a very important figure in the earliest history of the mission of the church, more important at this period than Peter, who has apparently not ventured beyond Jerusalem, or Paul, who was not yet even a Christian.

As in Samaria, Philip's witness in this passage is accompanied by wondrous events. That is typical of the apostolic witness in the New Testament. Not only does Acts report them, but Paul, in his own letters, refers to such wondrous events as a regular accompaniment of his mission activity (cf. Rom. 15:18-19; 2 Cor. 12:12). As is also typical of the apostolic witness in the New Testament, and emphasized in Acts, the whole episode is under the divine initiative begun at Pentecost with the coming of God's own Spirit upon the followers of Jesus Christ (e.g., 10:19; 13:2; 15:28; 16:6).

The "remembrance of things past" begins in the very first verse, where angelic instructions are given to Philip. As the activity of the Holy Spirit is described in ensuing verses, it is clear that we are meant to be reminded of the prophet Elijah, who received instructions in a similar way, and whose activity was accompanied by powerful manifestations of God's Spirit. There is some ambiguity in the Greek about Philip's instructions: The word used can mean either he is to go south to the road, or go to the road about midday. Since the Jerusalem-Gaza road ran in a southerly direction, it may be that Philip is given the time at which the chariot will pass on that road. In either case, the point is the same: Philip goes at angelic command, for a purpose he is not told, or at least we are not informed he was told.

The mission, as the text makes obvious, was to meet an Ethiopian official who had visited Jerusalem to worship, and who used his time returning to read the book of Isaiah. His native country symbolized power in the Old Testament (cf. Isa. 18:1-2), and is often coupled with Egypt to make that point (cf. Isa. 20:3-5; Ezek. 30:4-5). The fact that, although a eunuch, he had come to Jerusalem to worship, is itself an eschatological sign; eunuchs were forbidden such activity (Deut. 23:1) but in the new age even they would be welcome (cf. Isa. 56:3-5). Evidently such eschatological worship was already a reality; the new age is not solely promise. Its reality already impinges on the world.

That Philip heard the eunuch reading is not unusual (v. 30). At that time, all reading was vocalized, even that done privately. Philip's question and the Ethiopian's response reflect Acts' understanding of the way one comes to faith. Explanation of the Scriptures (here, of course, the Old Testament) to show they point to Jesus repeats the activity of the risen Jesus himself to two of his followers (Luke 24:27, 32), and thus represents the pattern for coming to faith. For what it is worth, this story in Acts is one of the few times this passage from Isaiah is applied to Christ in the New Testament (cf. 1 Pet. 2:21-25).

When therefore Philip instructs the eunuch about Christ on the basis of the Old Testament Scriptures (v. 35), he performs what Acts regards as the true apostolic witness. Peter preached that way (Acts 2:16-21; 3:18) as did Paul (13:27, 33-37; 17:2; see also Stephen [7:52] and Apollos [18:28]). The eunuch's request for baptism may reflect technical baptismal language; "Is there anything to *prevent* this person's baptism" may have been part of the early liturgy (cf. Acts 10:47; 11:17; Matt. 3:14; Mark 10:14). The addition of the baptismal confession in some later manuscripts (v. 37) may have occurred under the influence of such baptismal language.

Philip's transfer by the Spirit puts him in a direct line with Elijah (cf. 1 Kings 18:12; 2 Kings 2:16) and Ezekiel (Ezek. 3:14; 11:1). Thus Philip, who expounds the Old Testament, stands in a direct line with its prophetic figures. As it did them, the Spirit directs and empowers him as well. The Greek word for "spirit" is the same as for "wind," but this is not the gentle zephyr of a warm spring morning. It is the wind of limitless power that uproots trees, levels buildings, and drives the sea to towering fury. *That* is the divine power that guides the church and informs its message of God's saving grace in Jesus Christ.

Philip continued his Spirit-empowered preaching north along the coastal plain to Caesarea, where he may then have settled (see Acts 21:8). While we hear no more of his activity in Acts, his cognomen "the Evangelist" shows this was not the end of his activity. As is typical in Acts, what we get are glimpses of an episodic nature into the history of the early church rather than a total and complete narrative of everything that happened.

GOSPEL: JOHN 15:1-8

This passage from the Fourth Gospel is a continuation of Jesus' address to his disciples following his last meal with them during which the future traitor was identified (see 13:26-30). These chapters thus represent Jesus' final testimony to his closest followers and they contain, as one might expect, the essence of his message to them and to the world.

In the face of Jesus' impending death, his words give strong witness to the need of his disciples to remain united with him after his resurrection. Thus the continuing presence of the Holy Spirit is also implied in this passage, as it is made explicit in other parts of this final testimony.

The passage begins with one of the typically Johannine "I am" sayings. Several of those sayings that precede this one in John have associated Jesus with life: I am the bread of *life* (6:48); I am the resurrection and *the life* (11:25); I am the way, the truth, and *the life* (14:6). One could thus easily amplify this saying into "I am the vine [of life!]," since that is clearly what is implied in this figure of vine and branches. Just as the contact of the branch with the vine means life, and its separation death, so with the disciples and Jesus.

The figure of the vine is not accidental, especially not with the emphasis on Jesus as the *true* vine. The Old Testament is rich with imagery of Israel as a vine, both for good and ill. It is planted by God, a choice vine, but it has turned wild (Jer. 2:21; Isa. 5:1-7) and been ravaged by others (Ps. 80:8-19). In another vineyard parable, Jesus enlarged on the disobedience of Israel to the God who had established it (Mark 12:1-12). Thus Jesus and his followers represent as it were a replanting of the vine, this time of the true vine, that is, the vine that will not become wild and disobedient. But the origin of Jesus and his followers is the same as that of Israel; it is God who creates and tends his planting.

As in any vineyard, pruning must and will take place. For the disobedient, pruning is separation and death; for the obedient, pruning is for continued and greater fruit. But what could be interpreted as a prediction of suffering for unfaithful and faithful followers of Jesus alike is shown in following verse to be something else. It is Jesus' *words* that do the pruning. In the RSV, the same Greek word is translated "prune" in v. 2, and "made clean" in v. 3, but it would be clearer if the same translation were made in both verses. Then it would be clear that the "pruning" of v. 2 occurs by means of the "pruning" words of Jesus in v. 3. That in turn would make clear that it is the acceptance of Jesus' words that prunes and cleanses the branch/disciple, and leads to more fruit, just as it is the rejection of Jesus' words that separates for death (cf. 3:18, where acceptance or rejection of Jesus' words is already God's judgment). Thus union with Christ means in the first instance hearing and obeying his words, which for the Gospel of John is an excellent definition of "faith"!

With v. 5, a second theme is announced. The first theme was announced in 15:1: Christ is the vine whose Father, as caretaker, oversees it. The second theme in v. 5 develops what had already been discussed in the first four verses, namely, Christ is the vine and his disciples are the branches. The task is to remain in Christ, yet one cannot be united with someone who is absent. Thus, this passage implies the continuing presence of the divine Paraclete, which is discussed elsewhere in this same address of Jesus (cf. 14:26). Clearly, Jesus' execution does not mean permanent absence of the divine among human beings.

That one can do nothing apart from Christ (v. 5b) is also a Pauline theme, which he both states explicitly (see 2 Cor. 3:5) and develops by implication in the figure of the church as the body of Christ (see Rom. 12:4-5; 1 Cor. 12:12, 27). Just as separation from the vine means impotence here in John, so separation of the member from the body means impotence in Paul.

The fate of the unfruitful branches is to be gathered and burned (v. 6). While such language in the Bible is not unique to this passage (cf. Ezek. 15:1-8; Matt. 3:10; 7:19; 13:40-42) these are rather unliberal and arbitrary words Jesus speaks. Apart from him there is *only* destruction, just as he is not a way but *the* way, and not to just a god but to the *only* God. Apart from Jesus neither useful activity (v. 5b) nor existence (v. 6) is possible. It now begins to be clear why it is the words of Jesus that prune and cleanse, that unite with or separate from him. Only those who can accept such words, and hence such a Jesus, will abide in him and be his disciples.

It is in that light that v. 7 with its apparent "blank check" on divine power must be understood. Note well: The promise is to those who abide in Jesus, that is, those who hear and obey his words. The same point is made in 14:13-14, with the added phrase "in my name." Thus there, as here, what is asked is prompted by obedience to Jesus' own words. What we are promised is not "anything imaginable" but rather anything prompted and shaped by obedience to the words of Jesus. That kind of prayer will find its answer, because (v. 8) that kind of prayer glorifies the God who is the Father of Jesus, as he is then the Father of everyone who, abiding in Jesus and thus bearing fruit, proves to be his disciple.

SECOND LESSON: 1 JOHN 3:18-24

This passage serves virtually as a commentary on the verses from the Gospel of John. They carry forward the notion that one is united with Christ through obedience to his commands, and they identify the chief command as the one that concerns love.

The initial verse makes clear that the love about which the author writes is not so much a noun, and hence static, as it is a verb, and hence active. Note it is not "let us love *not only* by word *but also* by deed"; no such easy way out. Rather, "let us *not* love by word *but* by deed"; that apparently is the only way love can be done. Such acts must not only be done, they must be done "in truth." Truth is what distinguishes good from evil, because truth characterizes God, and what he does. Like love, truth in Johannine literature is not so much a noun as it is a verb. One not only knows the truth, one *does* the truth (1 John 1:6; 2:4; cf. John 3:21). Truth characterizes what God does, the God who is reliable and dependable and good. Such must deeds of love be also.

If love is basically a verb, that means it is not basically a feeling. That is perhaps the prevalent understanding of love in our culture, and it can do nothing but hinder an understanding of what the New Testament means by love. Love is an act for someone, not a feeling about someone. God loved the world not by getting all squishy inside at the thought of human beings; God loved the world by sending his Son to die for them. Love thus means an act for the good of another, and in a sense it must rise above emotions. We thus "love" our enemies not so much by *feeling* good about them as by *doing* something good for them, however we may happen to feel about them. Of course Christian love can include emotion, but it is not limited to, or limited by, emotions.

Well and good; love is an act. But how do we know what such acts of love are? What if it appears that our loving deeds are not accepted as such, or that they have not resulted in what in our view was good? The answer is: Have confidence in God because finally things are in his hands, not ours—no place here for tortured anxiety or paralyzing uncertainty. We are in God's hands and may safely act out his love for others in that confidence, a confidence in God, not in ourselves or our virtues.

In that confidence, we get what we ask (recall John 15:7), because, as those who keep God's commands delivered through his Son and thus do what he wants, we will ask for those things we know God wants us to have: active love for others. But by keeping his *commands* do we not fall back under law, and hence reliance on ourselves rather than on God? No, because God's command is precisely to trust in Christ, not in ourselves (v. 23). Such trust means we do what Christ asks of us, not because we trust ourselves, but because we trust him. Trust that does not obey, like love that does not act, is a self-contradiction. To trust is to commit self and acts to the one trusted. Such trust eventuates in acts of love for the community of trust; it eventuates in those acts that support and build up that community (cf. John 13:34).

And it is by such active, trusting love that we remain in Christ (v. 24). Proof of that remaining is the presence of God's Spirit, and the proof of the presence of the Spirit is the confession of Christ as Lord, something possible only by the power of that Spirit (cf. 4:2-3a, 13-15; 1 Cor. 12:3).

Such Spirit-empowered confession is finally the underlying reality which makes possible active love: trust in what God has done for us in his Son. God's Son is his active love; thus, seeing his Son in trust allows us to know what acts of love are, and gives us confidence to enact that love in obedience to the commands of the Son.

So we end as we began: The element that provides such unity as these three passages display is the power and presence of the Spirit of God. The similarity of content between the passage from the Gospel and First Epistle of John (especially the words about God granting whatever the disciple asks of him) make it clear that although the Spirit is not the focus of discussion in the Gospel passage, it presupposes the Spirit's reality and presence. That of course can be confirmed by a glance at the content of John 13–17, which represents the larger context of our passage. In many ways Gospel and epistle interlock, the epistle furnishing keys to the discussion carried on in the Gospel.

The power of that Spirit that is present with individual Christians and within their community of faith is made clear in the passage from Acts. By linking Philip to such Spirit-filled Old Testament prophets as Elijah and Ezekiel, Acts shows not only the power but the continuing guidance of that Spirit in the life of the church, a life that reaches back to that first community of faith, that first vineyard planted by God, namely his chosen people Israel. Truly the Spirit-filled Christian community stands in a goodly heritage, and awaits a splendid future!

The Sixth Sunday of Easter

Lutheran	Roman Catholic	Episcopal	Common Lectionary
Acts 11:19-30	Acts 10:25-26, 34-35, 44-48	Acts 11:19-30	Acts 10:44-48
1 John 4:1-11	1 John 4:7-10	1 John 4:7-21	1 John 5:1-6
John 15:9-17	John 15:9-17	John 15:9-17	John 15:9-17

The texts for this Sunday interlock in several ways. The passages from Acts and 1 John emphasize the Spirit of God, and the surprises and power it brings with it. The passages from John and 1 John emphasize the relationship between Christian love and obedience. All three texts bear witness to the nature of the Christian fellowship, reflecting the situation out of which they were written, and projecting for us the contours toward which we must strive in our effort to achieve genuine Christian fellowship. All three are thus to the point as the church journeys from the manifestation of God's power in his risen Son at Easter to the outpouring of that power in the Holy Spirit at Pentecost.

FIRST LESSON: ACTS 10:44-48

One is to expect surprises from the Holy Spirit. The Christian community was struggling with the realization that their crucified leader was now the risen Lord of glory, making them the heirs to the promises of Israel. Then on top of that the community is forced to confront the fact that Gentiles as well as Jews were heirs to those promises. It was this latter fact that was most difficult to understand, as the narrative of Acts makes clear.

What is surprising to Peter—that the Holy Spirit simply cannot wait for him to finish his sermon before it descends upon those who are listening—is also surprising to those who think there is a regular pattern in Acts: proclamation and confession of faith, then baptism and the coming of the Spirit. Here the Spirit descends prior to any confession of faith *or* act of baptism. The point is clear: The Spirit is in complete control of the life of the early church, and it refuses to abide by patterns either of ritual or of national origins. When proclamation of the story of Jesus is loose in the land, with its news of his cross (v. 39), his resurrection (v. 40), and his return in judgment (v. 42), one may expect surprises from the Holy Spirit!

This story is of extraordinary importance to modern Christians because this is the first time the Holy Spirit comes upon Gentiles, and the vast majority of modern Christians are of gentile, that is non-Jewish, ancestry. Only because of the event here recorded are we non-Jews allowed into the church. Peter's difficulty in understanding the point of his vision (Acts 10:9-19), which anticipated inclusion of non-Jews, shows how hard it was for those first Christians, all of Jewish background, to grasp that point. Yet whether they could grasp it or not, the Holy Spirit made it reality, and the church had to come to terms with it, hard as that was for some (see Acts 11:2; 15:1; Gal. 2:11-14).

What we have in this passage is, in a sense, the gentile Pentecost: The coming of the Spirit is accompanied by glossalia (v. 42; cf. 2:4), and by extolling or magnifying God and what he has done (the same root forms the noun in 2:11—"mighty deeds"—and the verb in 10:46—"magnifying"). The coming of the Spirit on Gentiles is thus demonstrated to be as genuine as its descent on the Jews in Jerusalem.

Peter's question in v. 47 again reflects liturgical language in regard to baptism with its use of the verb "to prevent" (on that point see the discussion of Acts 8:37 [Fifth Sunday of Easter]). Peter acknowledged the full validity of this bestowal of the Spirit both by declaring it had been given to Gentiles just as it had been given to Jews, and by remaining with the newly baptized gentile Christians for a period of time. Such fellowship between Jew and Gentile was challenged by some in the early church (see Acts 11:2; 15:1), and on occasion even Peter had difficulty living within it (see Gal. 2:11-14).

One final point: The descent of the Spirit on non-Jews is another of the events recorded in Acts that shows that the eschatological time foreseen by prophets had now become reality. This event fulfills the prophetic dream of the unity of all human beings who would share in the religious heritage of God's chosen people (see Isa. 66:18; Jer. 3:17; cf. also Mic. 4:2; Zech. 8:20-23). For that we gentile Christians may be profoundly grateful.

GOSPEL: JOHN 15:9-17

Whatever else this passage may convey, it makes abundantly clear that love and obedience to Jesus' commands are intimately intertwined. Love means to assume and carry out the obligations inherent in the Christian faith.

The passage also makes clear at its outset (v. 9) that Jesus is the incarnation of divine love. Jesus' love for humankind reflects the love of the Father for the Son. That is why Christians can have God as their Father, because he is first the Father of Jesus in his love for the Son, a love that the Son has then acted out toward us. Apart from Jesus, therefore, we do not have God as Father. Here is the ground of the divine fatherhood, in the essential relationship of Father and Son, not in some patriarchal image drawn from secular society. Moreover, only if we obey Jesus as he obeyed the Father can we remain in a relationship with God as our loving Father (cf. John 3:35-36).

Clearly enough, then, love means obedience (v. 10). Those who show obedience to Jesus as he showed obedience to God remain in a positive relationship, a relationship of love, to Jesus. Love is therefore the willing acceptance of divine discipline, not the absence of discipline (cf. John 14:15). Absence of divine discipline, as Paul affirms, is not the sign of God's love but rather of his wrath (see Rom. 1:24, 26, 28). God's grace has life-shaping power, and where that power is absent, so is grace, and where grace is absent, so is love.

Such Christian obedience is not onerous, however; it brings with it divine joy (v. 11), the joy Jesus has in his relation to the Father, and the joy we can have in our relation to Jesus. Yet the prerequisite of all joy is to know who one is and what one is to do. How much more then is it the prerequisite to divine joy! And we know who we are when we obey God's will as it is manifested in Jesus. That is why only there will true joy be found.

If, however, joy depends on obeying Jesus' commands, then the giving of those commands is a sheer act of love. And the gift of the command shares its content; together they give form to Christian love. Jesus' command is to love (v. 12), but more importantly, to love *as he loved.* That means that loving is a matter of giving, not getting; it means that loving is a matter of acting for the benefit and satisfaction of others, not ourselves. Love is thus not self-ish, it is self-giving, and only in that way can it be self-creating.

The measure and criterion of true love is therefore the cross of Jesus (v. 13)! It was there that Jesus made friends of those who had been the enemies of God; it was there that he made righteous followers out of those who before had been sinners (see also Rom. 5:6-8). It is on the cross, where Jesus laid down his life for others, that love is defined. Love is therefore in the first instance not a matter of words or of feelings, but of action.

If that is the case, then love demands an appropriate action as a response (v. 14). Jesus' self-giving love does not call us to bask in the warmth of self-acceptance; rather, it calls us to obey his words. If love is action, the loving response to such love must also be action. With such response we become friends of the crucified and risen Son of God.

To make that point, John uses the contrast of friend and slave (v. 15; the Greek word means just that; there is another word for hired servant, and that is not used here). A friend is one who knows another through and through. That is why a friend can obey out of love. A slave obeys out of fear of punishment: the master's command must be obeyed, whether understood or not.

That is not how we obey Jesus, our friend. We are not as slaves in our obedience to his commands. We obey as friends, friends with whom Jesus has shared the intimate secrets the Father has shared with him. That is another reason why Jesus is our access—our only access!—to that Father. We either know that Father through Jesus, or we do not know him at all (cf. 14:6).

Human reality—frail, rebellious, undisciplined reality—makes clear, however, that if our obedience even to Jesus our friend depended on our own strength, the command to love would be a curse. The call to obedience can be a call to joy only because that obedience does not come from our own resources. Above all the commands stands the love of Jesus who chose us before we were capable of choosing to follow him (v. 16). First John 4:19 says this in another way: "We love because he first loved us." So also here; we choose because he first chose us. We can obey him because he first established us on the sure ground of his love. We can bear fruit of obedience for him because he has opened our way to God, who alone can let us bear such fruit. And we can bear such fruit because through Jesus we are enabled to ask God to let us bear that fruit (on getting whatever we ask, see the comments on John 15:7, the Gospel for the Fifth Sunday of Easter).

Whatever else bearing fruit may mean, whatever other commands Jesus may give, this one stands out supreme: We are to love one another. We are to act for the good of the other, as Jesus acted for our good (see v. 13). Love is such action. Love is not only the kiss of peace, it is also the gift of food to the hungry sister. Love is not only the hearty handshake, it is also the time given in comfort of a grieving brother. Love is not only kind and supportive words, it is driving another on a necessary errand, or caring for another's children when an emergency arises, or giving time to comfort another who is in pain. With such actions we show love to the loving Savior who commands us to love one another.

SECOND LESSON: 1 JOHN 4:1-11

There is a sharp edge of reality to love, however. Love is more than simply the claim to love. Not everything that claims to be love is love, any more than everything that claims to be done in the name of or in the Spirit of Christ is done in obedience to him. There is a need to test those spirits that claim to impel in the name of Christ. Such testing was evident throughout the early church, since many who claimed Christian authority did so falsely (cf. 1 Thess. 5:19-21; Matt. 24:24; 2 Pet. 2:1). The final criterion that decides whether a spirit is from God is whether it conforms to the reality of Jesus.

And that points to a further problem: People were creating Jesus in their own image, tailoring the witness of Jesus to fit what they felt or wanted him to be. In their case, it was a Jesus who was far more divine than human, one who only *seemed* to be human (docetism, from Greek *dokeo,* to seem or appear). Such a divine phantom was more comfortable to their ideas of divinity, because then the divine Jesus didn't have to bother with such mundane things as eating or sleeping, or dying on a cross.

It would be nice to think that problem has disappeared, but it hasn't. It may take a different form, but people continue to try to shape Jesus in a way more comfortable to their ideas of what divinity is, or ought to be. If we accept the Jesus who told the story of the prodigal son, and ignore the Jesus who told the story condemning those who reject God's forgiving love (Matt. 18:23-35), we do not confess "Jesus according to the flesh," that is, the Jesus as he is really portrayed in the New Testament, our only source of reliable information about him. If we anticipate from Jesus only forgiving acceptance, whatever the act may be, but do not anticipate from him the kind of judgmental wrath he displays in Matt. 23:13-36, we do not confess the real Jesus. If we acknowledge only his peace, not his sword (Matt. 10:34); if we expect only affirmation from him, not also the rejection of those who reject him (Mark 8:38); if we want to hear him announce only acceptance, never punishment (Matt. 13:40-42; 25:46)—if that is the kind of Jesus we want to confess, then we do in fact not confess Jesus according to the flesh as that phrase is meant in this epistle.

In fact, this author goes further (v. 3): Not only do those who create Jesus in their own image of the divine not confess him correctly, they actually represent in themselves the forces arrayed against God and his Christ. They represent, in Johannine terms, the "world," and that means the "antichrist." To "deny Jesus come in the flesh" is in fact to oppose Jesus, to be in league with that final apocalyptic opponent of God and Jesus his Son.

The author knew a group who had tailored Jesus to their own pattern (v. 4). Perhaps they were other good "Christian" folk who just could not really believe Jesus did and said all those things that went against what a divine being really ought to have done and said. The great temptation, then and now, is to tailor the message of the tailored Christ so that it reflects the priorities of the society in which the church finds itself situated (v. 5). Cultural ideals—something like the absolute right of the individual to unrestricted choice in all matters, or the absolute inadmissibility of ethical absolutes—ideals represented by the "good" people in society, are baptized into the agenda of the church in an effort to get the world to pay attention.

Yet when the world does pay attention, when the culture finds its highest ideals affirmed by the pronouncements of the church, all that proves (v. 6) is that what the world is hearing is not the true Christian message, not the message of the risen Christ, illumined by the Spirit of the living, creating, and saving God. There is a criterion—an absolute criterion, if you will—by which to distinguish the divine from the profane spirit: Those who respond to the Jesus come in the flesh, with all the uncomfortable, unpopular, religiously insensitive things he had to say and do, like announcing moral absolutes, and claiming he was the *only* way to the true God—those are the true Christians. Those who reject such a Jesus for whatever reason—too culturally restricting, too judgmental, too time-conditioned—respond to that other spirit, that spirit which leads one away from God and his risen and regnant Son. Such people are to be rejected, if you please, for they do not confess the true Jesus "come in the flesh."

The fact that in this text the command to love (vv. 7-11) follows on the section about rejecting those who reject the true Jesus (vv. 1-6) shows that love without discerning judgment is a wicked, sentimental sham. Love that only affirms, whatever the act, and that does not judge and discipline, is not love at all. It is a sentimental aberration that does not take sin seriously, rather than a steely resolve to do what is best for the neighbor.

We must as Christians resist the temptation of sentimentalizing divine love (v. 8), as though anything *we* might want to identify as love were therefore necessarily divine in its origin and nature. Rather, here (v. 9) as always in the Johannine corpus, love must be defined by God's self-sacrificing gift of his only Son, and the Son's own life for the good of others, indeed for others who were in rebellion against him (v. 10). Yet if Jesus is the expression of God's love, then it is the Jesus who judged as well as loved, the Jesus who rejected as well as accepted, the Jesus who had hard words as well as the Jesus who affirmed others.

Love establishes relationships for the benefit of the other, and where the other does not benefit from the relationship, it is not true love. Yet benefiting another may not always mean the sentimental affirmation of what the other wants, however wrong, or perverse, or harmful that want may be. True love may need to wound in order to heal, but such love cannot come from us; it must start from God.

And start it God did, in his Son, and in all the Son did and said, and that fact lays upon the followers of that Son the necessity and the joy of sharing in such self-giving, other-benefiting love (v. 11). In the last analysis, that is the way the true Christian confession, "Jesus come in the flesh," is made real in the world of the flesh, the world which, left to itself, will oppose, and, if it could, destroy the love of that God and of his Son.

The Ascension of Our Lord

Lutheran	Roman Catholic	Episcopal	Common Lectionary
Acts 1:1-11	Acts 1:1-11	Acts 1:1-11	Acts 1:1-11
Eph. 1:16-23	Eph. 1:17-23	Eph. 1:15-23	Eph. 1:15-23
Luke 24:44-53	Mark 16:15-20	Luke 24:49-53	Luke 24:46-53 *or* Mark 16:9-16, 19-20

Ascension Day is the time when the church celebrates the limitless power of Christ given to him by God, a power used to overcome all other powers that would separate human beings from Christ as their Lord. The ascension of Christ is the penultimate act (the ultimate act is his return in glory) in the story of the transcendence of the divine plan over all limitations, moral or spiritual, that separate human beings from a loving relationship with God as their Creator and Father. In this instance, the author of Luke-Acts expresses that total transcendence in the form of the bodily ascension of Christ into heaven, thus demonstrating by such transcendence over physical forces his total transcendence over all spiritual forces as well. That transcendence is given nonpictoral explication in the passage from Ephesians.

GOSPEL: LUKE 24:44-53

We begin with the Gospel lesson, since it is an anticipatory summary of the fuller report of the ascension found at the beginning of the book of Acts. Luke clearly understands the ascension as the climax of Jesus' earthly career and the beginning of the church as witness to him. While Luke does not make explicit the idea that Jesus must leave before the Holy Spirit can come, as that is expressed in John 16:7, the order of events in Acts—ascension, Pentecost—clearly indicates he shared that theological view.

In the opening verse of this passage, Jesus makes explicit a major theological presupposition of Luke: Jesus is the fulfillment of God's self-revelation to his chosen people. That everything written by and about the chosen people and their fate is in the end also written about Jesus is clear attestation to his preeminent status with God. All three categories of Jewish Scripture are included here: Torah (Pentateuch) Nebi'im (Prophets) and Kethubim (Writings). Nothing of Scripture is foreign to its final fulfillment in Christ. The necessity of that fulfillment is the divine necessity: so God himself had planned it. All is finally in God's hands; that is a constant theme in the New Testament.

Jesus now does (v. 45) for all the apostles what he had done for the two on the road to Emmaus (24:27). Thus what was formerly impossible (see Luke 9:45) now by the direct act of Christ becomes possible: They can now understand Scripture. It is no wonder then that such christocentric interpretation of Scripture becomes a central mode of missionary witness in the early church (cf. Acts 17:2; 18:28).

What Luke has in mind (v. 46) is not some general understanding of Scripture, however. The understanding is quite specific: Scripture illumines how the Passion of Christ and his death on the cross were not accidental, an unfortunate incident where an innocent person was caught up in a miscarriage of justice played out against the canvas of larger events in the Roman domination of Palestine. Rather, that event was in accord with God's plan. The cross is therefore not defeat, but victory for that plan, as the resurrection and ascension then make plain. This was also the point of Jesus' three prophecies about himself (Luke 9:22; 17:25; 18:32-33), which also were not understood when they were delivered (cf. 18:34; 24:45), even though those prophecies also reflected the divine necessity of God's plan.

More specifically, it is difficult to know which, if any, specific Old Testament passages the gospel traditions had in mind when they refer to these prophecies of what had to happen to the Christ. Hosea 6:2 is often cited by scholars; Jesus himself interpreted Jonah 1:17 as such a prophecy according to Matt. 12:39-40. Perhaps they thought in a more general way that as God had directed the course of his chosen people, so he brought it to fulfillment in Christ.

With vv. 46-47 we get what is essentially a summary of the apostolic preaching in Acts, which regularly contains these elements of witness to Christ from the Old Testament, his death and resurrection, and the call to repentence. The command to preach to all nations is also found in Matt. 28:19-20, and in Mark 16:16-17, although the latter verses, which appear only in later manuscripts of Mark, are probably derived from our passage and the wording of Matthew. They are also reflected in Acts 5:31-32 and 17:30, showing the divine origin of the apostolic proclamation in Acts.

It is also important to note that the command to go to all nations shows that the gentile mission, so contested in the early church (see Acts 11:1-3; 15:1), was part of the intention of the risen Jesus himself. Yet that did not exclude the Jews; the mission was to begin with them in Jerusalem (cf. Rom 1:16; 2:9-10).

In v. 49 we have an anticipatory summary of the story beginning in Acts 1:4. None of what Jesus has just commanded, of which the apostles are to be the witnesses (v. 48), can be carried out without direct divine assistance. Just as Jesus' career was in direct accord with the divine plan (v. 44), so will the course of the church be. It will be directed by God's own Spirit. Thus both past and future lie equally in God's hands and are equally at his disposal.

The chronology contained in Luke 24:1, 13, 33 implies that the ascension occurred on Easter Sunday, not after a forty-day period as in Acts 1:3. It shows the general meaning of "forty days" in Acts (see comments below on Acts 1:3). The important point here is Jesus' final act of blessing, mentioned both in vv. 50 and 51. It is his final blessing on the apostolic mission, which thus fulfills God's plan, has the blessing of the Son, and is directed by the power of the Holy Spirit.

Significantly, the first act of the apostles is one of obedience (v. 52): They do what Jesus told them to do (v. 49). Their joy is a regular concomitant of faith in the early church, even when Christians underwent persecution (cf. Matt. 5:11-12; Col. 1:24; James 1:2; 1 Pet. 1:6; 4:13). Since Christianity was the fulfillment of the plan God began with his chosen people, it was natural that the earliest Christians, beginning with the apostles on their return to Jerusalem, would participate fully in the devotion of the chosen people to that God. Temple worship was thus a regular practice of those first Christians (cf. Acts 2:46; 3:1; 5:42). It continued to the very end of the period narrated in Acts: When Paul returns for the last time to Jerusalem, he participates in temple ritual (21:26). Only with the destruction of the temple in A.D. 70 did this practice apparently cease.

FIRST LESSON: ACTS 1:1-11

In these verses, Acts announces itself as the second volume of a work about what Jesus said and did. These verses, coupled with the closing verses of Luke, provide enough of a link to get the continuation of the story under way. That Luke is described as dealing with what Jesus "began to do and teach" (Acts 1:1) implies that the apostles, empowered by God's Spirit, will continue that work.

The Theophilus to which the work is addressed is otherwise unknown. His name means "friend of God" and could thus be an ideal reader as well as a patron who would take responsibility for distributing Luke-Acts. Since nothing further is known, it is probably better not to make too much of him in the exegesis of Acts.

The "apostles" whom Jesus chose are the twelve (cf. Luke 6:13). The term *apostle,* with minor exceptions, is limited in Luke-Acts to the twelve disciples. The language of v. 2 is confessional in tone (cf. 1 Tim. 3:16) and may even reflect the assumption of Elijah into heaven (cf. 2 Kings 2:11); in Luke, Jesus, not John the Baptist, reflects Elijah.

The "many proofs" (v. 3) that Jesus was alive are probably not miraculous signs; they more probably refer to such events as that recorded in Luke 24:41-43, where Jesus proved he was not the phantom or apparition the apostles had first thought. The forty-day period is a traditional period of time, as shown by Luke 4:2; it means a relatively extended but indeterminate period, as Acts 13:31 indicates. It is the period of time, however, by which the church calculates the day of the ascension. It falls on the fortieth day after Easter, Easter Sunday itself being included in the reckoning.

The real importance of the verse is the content of Jesus' instruction. Mention of the kingdom of God brackets the entire book of Acts; it is the last thing reported of Paul's preaching in Rome (28:31). Thus Luke leaves no doubt about the reality that underlies the narrative that is contained within those brackets: It is a divine, not a merely human, reality about which he is reporting.

The promise contained in vv. 4-5 (in Luke 3:16 it is attributed to John the Baptist; in Acts 11:16, Peter remembers Jesus also spoke it) is repeated in v. 8, thus indicating its importance. That importance is also borne out in the narrative of Acts itself. Prior to the empowerment by the Holy Spirit, there is no proclamation, no witnessing to Jesus anywhere. But while there is no evangelizing prior to Pentecost, it begins *immediately* thereafter (see 2:14). Since there is no report the disciples were ever given a water baptism by Jesus, this promised baptism cannot represent some kind of necessary "second baptism" by the Spirit. It is the only baptism the Twelve receive in Luke-Acts.

The apostles' question about restoring the kingdom to Israel reflects the prophetic hope that one day all nations would serve Israel (cf. Zech. 14:16-18); dreams of political glory die hard. The disciples desire a timetable (cf. Luke 19:11); they want to walk, as it were, by sight rather than by faith. Jesus will have none of it (v. 7). It is enough to know that God is in control; to know the kind of date the apostles desire would be to know more than God's angels or the Son himself knows (cf. Matt 24:36).

The important point is the gift of the Spirit that empowers a universal mission (v. 8). The descent of that Spirit is a further mark of the eschatological times inaugurated by the appearance, and especially the resurrection, of Jesus (cf. Joel 2:28-32, so interpreted in Acts 2:17-21; Isa. 32:15-17).

That Jesus' ascension is a divine act is shown by the presence of the cloud, a typical biblical figure for God's presence (e.g. Exod. 13:21; 24:15-18; Luke 9:34-35). The presence of the two men is further indication of the divine importance of the event; such angelic presence is noted only at climactic events (conception of John [Luke 1:11] and of Jesus [1:26]; Jesus' birth [2:9, 13]; his resurrection [24:4]; his ascension [Acts 1:10]). Therefore the ascension means assuming divine power over the course of the world and its history (cf. 1 Pet. 3:22). The announcement of his return in the power of God (v. 11; "in the same way" refers to the cloud, and hence the divine nature of that return) means that the church, empowered by God's Spirit, lives in the interim between the ascension and return of Jesus, and hence lives for and by the grace of God alone.

SECOND LESSON: EPHESIANS 1:15-23

This passage is an appropriate commentary on the meaning of the ascension. It speaks of Christ's transcendent power over creation; he has become the Lord of power over time and eternity, in accordance with the plan of God. The passage itself is characterized by a liturgical redundancy (see esp. vv. 17, 19, 23), which gives it a solemn tone and puts the statements about the overpowering superiority of Christ into a context of worship, the only context appropriate for such a discussion.

Further indication of worship as the context is the fact that the passage is a prayer on behalf of the recipients of the letter, a regular feature of the apostolic epistle (cf. Rom. 1:8; 1 Cor. 1:4; Col. 1:3-4, 9; Philem. 4-5). The language shows the readers are not known in person to the author; hence if it was written by Paul it was not to Ephesus, if to Ephesus it was not by Paul. In the end, however, that is of minor import. The church has recognized in this letter an expression of the apostolic faith that underlies the church of Jesus Christ, whoever the author may have been. It is better therefore to spend energy on understanding the message rather than on trying to prove or disprove Pauline authorship.

Unceasing prayer of the kind represented in this passage is part of the apostolic commission (v. 16). It is interesting to note that the only help

Paul desired from the Romans in his time of potential trouble in Jerusalem was their prayers (Rom. 15:30-31), so powerful did he think prayer to be. Such unceasing prayer for all peoples everywhere is a task sadly neglected by most modern Christians.

The divine granting of wisdom and knowledge is a part of the eschatological age in Isa. 11:2, and is probably also so understood here in v. 17. The one who grants those gifts remains God himself, not the Son. The ultimate subordination of the Son to the Father is typical of Pauline theology (cf. esp. 1 Cor. 15:28), a subordination that in no way diminishes the glory and power of the Son, however, as vv. 20-22 in our passage make clear. The central actor remains, however, the Father, who begets the Son and sends the Spirit to fulfill his plan.

One of the major results for the followers of the ascended and reigning Christ is a new future, as they look forward to the new world Christ will inaugurate with his return. One of the characteristic ways of expressing that new future is in terms of new birth, and of the new inheritance such a new birth would bring. That theme is touched on in v. 18; for a fuller explication of that thought see 1 Pet. 1:3-9. The point is that the reality which becomes visible for all to see in the new age is already present within the community of those baptized into Christ. Because the same God who raised Christ from the dead has promised Christ will return in glory, the Christian can be filled with hope. All of this together points to the new inheritance the Christians share now, and look forward to sharing in a fuller way in the future (cf. Col. 1:5, 27; Rom. 9:23; Acts 20:32; Heb. 9:15). This verse thus shares the common early Christian terminology that expressed the "already" in the presence of the Spirit in the community of the faithful, and the "not yet" of the final transformation of reality to be inaugurated with the return of Christ.

The redundant language used to express the greatness of God's power (v. 19; cf. 3:20) is an attempt to express in finite language the infinite power of the Creator. Such attempts would be hopelessly abstract were it not for the fact that the supreme expression of that power is the raising of Christ from the dead (v. 20; cf. Rom. 4:24; 8:11; 2 Cor. 13:4; Col. 2:12; 1 Pet. 1:21). That historic fact is the rock on which all Christian formulations of divine omnipotence must be grounded. As this verse in Ephesians shows, the resurrection is completed by the ascension to "the right hand" of God. That is the position of honor and power. In classical theological language, the *sessio ad dextram* is the root of all expressions about *christos pantocrator.*

Thus, the ascension of Christ and his being seated at God's right hand means Christ is now the supreme power over all space and time. The list of powers over which Christ rules is not exhaustive but exemplary (v. 21; for other such lists, see 2:2; 3:10; 6:12; Rom. 8:38; 1 Cor. 15:24; Phil. 2:9-10; Col. 1:16; 2:15; 1 Pet. 3:22); it intends to say that there is no power, natural or supernatural, that falls outside the ruling power of Christ risen and regnant. This subordination of all created reality to Christ is also typical of early Christian theology (cf. Acts 2:33; 1 Cor. 15:25), and is here (v. 22) expressed in terms of Ps. 8:6, as it is in 1 Cor. 15:27.

The astonishing fact, and the fact that gives the ascension of Christ its grip on our own reality, is that this inexpressible, limitless power by which Christ rules over the whole of created reality, spiritual and material, is to be found in the church when it praises Christ as Lord and does his will. Just as Christ now possesses full divine power over all of reality, so that full power is now at work in and through the church, to bring about the confession of Christ as Lord by all peoples everywhere. Thus the ascension commands and empowers the universal proclamation of the gospel, and gives that responsibility to the church here and now.

The Seventh Sunday of Easter

Lutheran	Roman Catholic	Episcopal	Common Lectionary
Acts 1:15-26	Acts 1:15-17, 20a, 20c-26	Acts 1:15-26	Acts 1:15-17, 21-26
1 John 4:13-21	1 John 4:11-16	1 John 5:9-15	1 John 5:9-13
John 17:11b-19	John 17:11b-19	John 17:11b-19	John 17:11b-19

The unity of these three passages centers on Christian life and discipleship within the matrix of the community of the faithful. The passage from Acts describes the apostolic foundation of that community; that foundation with its twelve members replicates the foundation of the twelve tribes of the Israel it fulfills. With that foundation, the church is then ready for the empowering event of Pentecost to launch it on its world-encircling mission. The epistle shows the inner reality of that community, based as it is on willing acceptance of God's witness to his Son as the one in whom alone we may have true life. The Gospel, a portion of Jesus' "High Priestly

Prayer," displays the reality of the community in the midst of a hostile world, showing how its founder, Jesus, had already anticipated and provided for survival in such a negative environment. The last Sunday before Pentecost thus anticipates the empowering of the community of the faithful by God's own Spirit, so it may proclaim the living reality it knows within and among its members.

FIRST LESSON: ACTS 1:15-26

This passage, like so much in Acts, is deliberately cast in the form of fulfillment of the Old Testament (e.g., v. 16). Luke casts it in that form to make clear his view that God is in total control, through his Spirit, of the career and fate of the church. Such control is demonstrated by the fact that all occurs within the plan of God announced beforehand in the Scriptures of the chosen people Israel.

The Twelve who constituted Jesus' inner circle of followers had originally been named by Jesus early in his public career (Luke 6:13-16; their names are again recited in Acts 1:13 by way of reminder to the readers of this two-volume work). They were chosen from among the larger number that followed Jesus; Luke declares Jesus "called his disciples and chose from them twelve, whom he named apostles," thus indicating the distinction between "disciple" and "apostle" he maintains through both volumes of his work. The fact that a replacement must be named for Judas, whose defection reduced the number to eleven, shows the significance of the number twelve. It is interesting to note that while all Gospels agree on the number, they do not agree on the names, itself a silent witness to the importance of their number, which transcends the importance of the individuals who constitute it.

The fact that Peter initiates the process of choice (v. 15) shows his status as *primus inter pares* (first among equals) from the outset of the church. He has that status most probably on the strength of his being the first one to whom the risen Jesus appeared (cf. Luke 24:34; 1 Cor. 15:5; in John 20:11-16 that honor goes to Mary Magdalene, while Peter is the first to enter the empty tomb). The notation that there were about 120, many of whom had been disciples from the outset of Jesus' career (cf. vv. 21-22), shows there was a considerable number from which to choose the apostle to complete the circle of twelve.

Typical of the speeches in Acts, this speech by Peter sets forth the way Luke wishes us to understand the events he records. Peter's first words enunciate the principle that what is occurring fulfills Scripture, and therefore God's will, and thus shows that the driving force behind these events is

God himself. The specific Scripture alluded to here is most likely Ps. 41:9, a passage quoted directly in this connection in John 13:18, and perhaps alluded to as well in Mark 14:18. That betrayal by a member of the inner circle (v. 17) is a well-known theme from folk literature does not lessen its tragedy in this context.

The account of the death of Judas rehearsed by Peter (v. 18) implies accidental death; in the only other account of his death, a remorseful Judas hanged himself (Matt. 27:4-5). In Acts there is no remorse; his death is a kind of poetic justice. He meets his death on the land purchased with the fee he got for betraying Jesus to his death! The one detail of his death is ambiguous; it can mean either Judas "(fell) headlong" or "prone," or it could mean "swollen up" (perhaps from disease). The other detail, that he "burst open," is compatible with either of those two possible meanings.

Judas' bloody death gave the place its name, the Aramic *Akeldama*. Matthew has a different account: The field, named perhaps for the profession of a former owner, "Potter's Field," became a burial ground for strangers. The lack of certainty about such details as Judas' death or the name of the field he had purchased shows the danger of seeking to put primary emphasis on detailed historical accuracy in such accounts, thereby ignoring the larger theological point such stories are intent on making.

Again, the betrayer's fate, as his betrayal, had been in accord with the divine plan, demonstrated by the quotations from Ps. 69:25 and 109:8. Psalm 69, along with Psalm 22, helped shape the accounts of Jesus' crucifixion in the Gospels, and its popularity in early Christian circles is shown here in Acts as well.

The qualifications for "apostle" (vv. 21-22) give us more insight into Luke's theological understanding of the early church than they give us historical detail. For Luke, the name "apostle" is reserved for the Twelve, and to be one of the Twelve, one must have accompained Jesus from the beginning of his public career (cf. John 15:27). For that reason, with one minor exception (Acts 14:14), Luke does not refer to Paul as an apostle. Paul, on the other hand, defines an apostle as one who had seen the risen Lord (1 Cor. 9:1a) and had been commissioned to preach a church-founding gospel (Gal. 1:16; 1 Cor. 9:1b-2; cf. also Matt. 28:19-20). Both Luke and Paul agree, however, that the primary function of an apostle is to witness to the risen Christ. For Luke, the announcement of that witness is a regular element of apostolic preaching (cf. Acts 2:32; 3:15; 4:33; 5:32; 10:41; 13:31); for Paul, denial of Jesus' resurrection is a denial of the fundamental element of the Christian faith (1 Cor. 15:14, 17).

How the candidates were narrowed to the two men, Joseph and Matthias, (v. 23) is not known, nor is anything known about the men themselves from the New Testament record. Nor is either one mentioned subsequently in the account in Acts. Those facts point again to the symbolic significance of the number twelve, more important than the individuals who constituted that group. Indeed, the hero of the second half of Acts, Paul, was not even a member of it.

The apostolic prayer (vv. 24-25) shows the final choice is God's, and hence gives the theological rationale of casting lots (cf. Prov. 16:33). The practice goes back to the Old Testament, where the tribes of Israel were assigned their land by lot (cf. Num. 26:55; Josh. 14:1-2) and their first king, Saul, was chosen the same way (1 Sam. 10:20-21). Thus in the story of Israel, as in that of the early church, at key points the divine initiative in its ongoing story is made clear.

The filling out of the Twelve is the extent of the activity open to the church prior to Pentecost. After the descent of the Holy Spirit, there will be no time for such internal housekeeping. At that point, and from then on, all energy is devoted to external evangelization. There is a lesson here the modern, post-Pentecost church would do well to learn: Contemporary preoccupation with internal structures within and among denominations shows the church has regressed to a pre-Pentecostal state.

GOSPEL: JOHN 17:11b-19

These verses represent the central part of what has come to be known as Jesus' "High Priestly Prayer" (ch. 17), although it is nowhere so designated in the Fourth Gospel. It represents a reprise of what Jesus, in obedience to the Father, has done. It also explicates the close link between the career and fate of Jesus and that of his followers.

The intent of the prayer is not the unity of humanity as such, and surely not of the unity of church and world; v. 9 makes clear that the concern of the prayer is specifically not the world. Rather it is the unity of the followers of Christ, as they are defined in John 17:8. The thrust of the chapter is the church over against an alien, disbelieving world: The only way the church can survive in such a world is to be united within itself, and with Christ. That danger is that they must now continue in the world even after Jesus has left it (v. 11a).

Such continuance will depend on the unity of the community of faith being grounded in the unity of the Son with the Father (v. 11b; cf. John 10:30), and of Christians with both divine persons (cf. also vv. 21-23). Up to the point of the prayer, Jesus' physical presence has protected the unity and safety of his followers. The defection of Judas is only an apparent exception, since his betrayal was part of God's plan and had been announced in Scripture (v. 12; see also the discussion of Acts 1:15-26 above).

Such unity, grounded in Jesus' words, is the source of joy for his followers (v. 13; cf. 15:11). Such joy is a regular Johannine theme: true joy is that which comes from hearing and accepting the words of Jesus. The dark side of such joy is the fact that it is met by hate on the part of those who do not accept Jesus' words (v. 14). It is the character of the "world" to reject and hate what Jesus represents. That "world" for John is the reality that prefers darkness to light (cf. 3:19), lies to truth (cf. 8:44), and that therefore will have nothing to do with Jesus, who is himself light and truth. It is because Jesus' followers accept him as the exclusive way to the Father that the "world" hates them, as it had also hated Christ (cf. 15:18).

Yet the survival of the church depends not on a withdrawal from that world, or from contact with it (v. 15), but rather on protection from the ravages of that world, and from the Evil One who rules it and whose desire it enacts. In contrast to that world, Jesus and his followers have a wholly other point of origin (v. 16). For that reason, participating in Jesus and participating in the world represent two irreconcilable modes of existence.

The only way the church can be protected from that world and its destructive intent vis-à-vis the church is to be sanctified by God. To be "sanctified" here as always means to be set apart by God for his own purposes. Jesus' followers are thus to be in but not of the world (cf. also Rom. 12:2). Such sanctification will and does occur through God's Word *(logos!)*, who, of course, is Jesus. Thus Jesus is the divine word by which Christians are set apart by God for his own purposes in the world. And Jesus' words are true because he himself is truth, just as his words are divine because he himself is divine.

The purpose of such sanctification is made clear in v. 18: Participation in fellowship with Jesus and through him with the Father is for the purpose of announcing God's truth to the world. Not only is the church not to withdraw from contact with the world, it is to move into the world, into the midst of those whose lethal hate is spewed out against them. The followers of Jesus, and through him of the Father, are to "shine as lights in the midst of the perverse and crooked generation" (cf. Phil. 2:15). Just as God sent his Son into a hostile world (cf. John 1:9-11), so the Son sends his followers, and for the same purpose: to gather together those who accept Jesus as their Lord (cf. 1:12-13). Thus the prayer of Jesus sums up and demonstrates the realities announced in the Johannine prologue.

Furthermore, this sanctification of Christians is derived from the sanctification of the Son, represented by his death for the world (v. 19; Jesus' "hour" mentioned in 17:1 is in John the hour of his death). That death makes possible participation in God's truth despite the hostile environs of the world. As the next verses (20-21) will make clear, such participation will be extended and enlarged even after Jesus has returned to the Father, and is no longer visibly present in the world. In that way, God uses the persecution and death of Jesus to set forth his purposes; Christians may thus have confidence that God will continue to use the persecution of the Christians to set forth his purposes as well.

SECOND LESSON: 1 JOHN 5:9-15

There is a stark, even offensive, simplicity to this passage, whose key is v. 12: With the Son there is life, without him only death. No further qualifications, no further considerations, no subtlety, no complexities: With the Son, we have God, and therefore life, glorious life now and in the age to come; without the Son, we have death, that and naught else.

There is a compactness to the argument of v. 9 because there is an unspoken member of the argument. The "if" assumes the reality of the condition; it could as well be translated "since." The argument in full seems to be: Since we are willing to accept human witness, we ought also accept the divine witness, the more so since God is greater than human beings, and therefore his witness is more likely to be true.

Yet more: The witness itself is greater. That witness consists in Scripture (cf. John 5:39b), John the Baptist (cf. John 5:33), and the things Jesus does and says (cf. John 5:36). All of this points to one crucial fact: God sent his Son. The Son is not a social, or biological, or human religious phenomenon; the Son is sent by God himself.

To reject that fact is to reject what God himself has said about his Son (v. 10). To accept it is to take the witness to the core of our lives, and let it be the source of our own deeds and words (cf. John 3:33). Furthermore, not to trust and thus accept this witness about the Son is not only passively to turn away from God, it is also actively to make God a liar. Thus we reject the One who comes to us in Christ as our friend (cf. Rom. 5:10) and tell him we prefer to have him as our enemy, since he is a liar about his Son.

The witness we thus reject is more than merely words, and therefore its consequences are more than simply intellectual (v. 11). The witness is quite literally a matter of life and death, and life of a wholly new quality, at that. The Greek word usually translated "eternal" is an adjectival form of the word for "eon" or "age" and refers to the new age of transformed reality. The emphasis is thus on life which shares the quality of the new age, rather than on its duration. After all, life such as we know it, with all its pain and suffering, which would then simply not end would not be much of a gift! That is why one can have life that shares in the quality of the new eon (that is, life in the grace-filled presence of God) even now, and hence in that way transcend death. That is why even though we die, yet we live, live now with Christ in the quality of the life to come. Such life is available only in the Son of God. Apart from that Son there is only darkness, loneliness, pain, and death.

Thus v. 12 is the climax. Here is the simple yet terrifying consequence of all this: To have the Son and therefore God who is the author of life is to have that life for ourselves. Not to have the Son is not to have God and hence not to have that life. That is the summary capstone of the epistle (see 1 John 5:20) as it is of the Gospel (see John 20:31); all else is commentary.

The striking fact in all this is that this life of the future age can begin now (v. 13)! The quality of life in the new age already shines through the joy of the worshiping community. To announce and affirm that reality is the point of this letter, as it is of the entire New Testament. Those who trust, and hence accept, and therefore shape their lives on the fact that in Jesus we have to do uniquely with God, already share the shape of life in the age to come, with its universal acclamation of Christ as Lord, and its universal light and joy and peace.

Within the reality of that new life, we have the freedom and boldness to ask confidently for the spread of that reality to all peoples, which reflects God's will in sending his Son. To such requests God will surely listen, indeed listen attentively. In such prayers, therefore, we ourselves are included in the powerful fulfillment of the divine will.

Such is our confidence, and such the reliability of God, that to ask is to receive (v. 15), so ready is God to shower on us the benefits of the new life he desires us to have in his Son. All prayer made in accord with the will of the Father is to be made in the confidence that its utterance assures its fulfillment. Such prayer shares already in the reality of the age to come.

The Day of Pentecost

Lutheran	Roman Catholic	Episcopal	Common Lectionary
Ezek. 37:1-14	Acts 2:1-11	Acts 2:1-11 *or* Isa. 44:1-8	Acts 2:1-11 *or* Ezek. 37:1-14
Acts 2:1-21	1 Cor. 12:3b-7, 12-13	1 Cor. 12:4-13 *or* Acts 2:1-11	Rom. 8:22-27 *or* Acts 2:1-21
John 7:37-39a	John 20:19-23	John 20:19-23 *or* John 14:8-17	John 15:26-27; 16:4b-15

What unites these passages is their various comments on the effects of the Holy Spirit on the lives of God's people in past, present and future. Each passage is so rich that a sermon could easily be devoted to it alone; altogether they provide the preacher with an embarrassment of riches for preaching on the day that commemorates the empowerment of the community of the faithful for their task of incorporating in word and deed the grace of God showered on sinful humanity in the Lord Jesus Christ.

FIRST LESSON: EZEKIEL 37:1-14

The story is told with graphic detail: The prophet is taken to a valley, where the sun bounces off the canyon walls to parch the valley floor. There he sees a field of bones, very dry bones, dry as only old bones can be, weathered in sun and rain, parched and cracked. On the command to reassemble, there is even a sound of rattling, but then what else would happen when parched, weathered, dry old bones start to move, and bump into each other as they find their correct places after all those years of dislocation? Ezekiel lets us not only see, but hear this astounding work of the Lord!

There are many aspects to this account. The story is a story of the power of God's creative word—the power of the word by which he created the universe in the first instance is repeated here. If in that first creation he breathed life into clay, here he recreates human beings from parched bones. It is the power of God's Word that created human beings, and then here recreates them.

It is the same powerful Word by which God led a captured people out of Egypt, and made of that band of slaves a nation, a people for his peculiar possession, a nation of priests, and a holy nation. Israel in Egypt was about as promising a material for a people of God as a valley full of old, parched, very dry bones.

Yet more: It is the same powerful Word, incarnated in Jesus of Nazareth, through whom God re-created, renewed, and redeemed the human race, who made of them in his Son a new kingdom of priests and a holy nation, and made a redeemed people from a human race that was about as promising as a parched valley full of very dry old bones.

Clearly enough, in this story Israel is the dry bones—Israel in exile, sent into slavery for her sins against God, Israel who has resisted repenting. Of them God said, through Isaiah: "This people's wits are dulled, their ears are deafened and their eyes blinded, so that they cannot see with their eyes nor listen with their ears nor understand with their minds, so that they may turn and be healed" (cf. Isa. 6:9-10). Yet even such people, God tells Ezekiel in his vision, are not beyond the reach of God's saving, empowering Spirit. If dry bones can live, so can God's people, vivified by his powerful Spirit. That is the Spirit that comes, and empowers the church, at Pentecost.

SECOND LESSON: ACTS 2:1-21

As Peter's speech makes clear, the Pentecost event is proleptic eschatological fulfillment. The presence of the Spirit promised by the prophet Joel in the past is a guarantee of a future transformed reality. Fire and Spirit on Jesus' followers fulfills his word in Luke 24:49 (cf. Acts 1:8), and the Baptist's word in Luke 3:16. Speaking in tongues is a sign of the presence of God's Spirit (cf. Acts 10:46; 19:6), but not a necessary one (cf. Acts 8:17; 1 Cor. 12:30, where the Greek expects the answer "no" to each question). All who have the Spirit may speak in tongues (1 Cor. 14:5) but there are more important things for them to do (1 Cor. 14:19).

In this passage, tongues are understood to mean foreign languages; thus vv. 7-11 foreshadow the universal mission of the church (see v. 17, quoting Joel who announces the Spirit coming upon "all flesh"; cf. also Isa. 2:2-3). The confusion and misunderstanding wrought by human rebellion at Babel (Gen. 11:1-9) is here overcome by the unifying power of the Holy Spirit.

Not all understand these languages, however; divine phenomena are always capable of another interpretation. We do in fact continue to walk by faith, not sight! Similarly, only as Christian experience is interpreted by Scripture (cf. v. 16) can we be sure it is the work of the Holy Spirit. To judge Scripture by our experience is to stand with those who jeered at Pentecost (v. 14). Thus the first part of Peter's sermon interprets this experience in light of Scripture, and states, in the final verse from Joel (Acts 2:21), the basic thrust of the apostolic proclamation (cf. 4:12): Only Spirit-empowered people who confess Jesus as Lord can be delivered in the final judgment.

EPISTLE: ROMANS 8:22-27

The presence of God's Spirit among Christians is a guarantee of the reality of God's future redemptive transformation of reality, and our participation in it. The Spirit is the first fruits of a greater harvest yet to come. God's Spirit among us at once intensifies our yearning to be delivered from the present rebellious age, and makes that same world bearable because we know it is not God's final act. God by his Spirit guarantees the followers of Christ a better future, to come in his own good time.

The childbirth imagery of v. 22 is usual for the sufferings that are to presage and accompany such a redemptive transformation of reality (cf. Isa. 13:8; 1 Thess. 5:3; 1 Enoch 62:4). The pain of the birth of that new reality brings a joy comparable to that of the birth of a child. Only the presence of the Spirit makes those woes bearable; by that presence we know already the new reality (v. 23). But it also makes them more difficult to bear, since we already know the new reality and yearn the more for its speedy coming. Its essential futurity is shown by the accompanying "redemption of our bodies" (for what that means, see 1 Cor. 15:42-54).

That future hope is such a vivid reality for Paul that in the context of that future hope he can, for the only time in his letters, refer to being saved in the past tense (v. 24). It remains the future consummation that saves us (see Rom. 5:10, 17; 6:5, 8; 8:11), however confident we may be of our participation in it because of God's grace in Christ.

Until that consummation, the manifestation of salvation is patient waiting in the secure knowledge that God is in control, and will act to redeem his creation (v. 25). In the meantime, the Spirit maintains our contact with God through prayer (vv. 26-27). The sin that blocks such communication is overcome by the presence of the Spirit, which is another current manifestation of salvation from a sinful world. Such prayer by the Spirit for us and through us is in accord with God's will; in fact, God gave his Spirit for just such activities (v. 27). Just as in Acts there can be no preaching apart from the Spirit—preaching does not begin in that story until Pentecost—so here there can be no prayer apart from that Spirit. All of that means simply that apart from the Spirit, there can be no church at all.

GOSPEL: JOHN 15:26-27; 16:4b-15

In this passage, the theological assumption that underlies the narrative in the first two chapters of Acts—first Jesus' ascension, then the coming of the Holy Spirit—is here made explicit (cf. also 15:7). Indeed, as Acts makes clear by the fact that there is no Christian witness until the coming of the Spirit at Pentecost, Christian witness depends on the prior witness of God to himself by the Holy Spirit (John 15:27).

The second portion of the reading from John (16:4b-15) is the final promise of the "Paraclete" (= Advocate, Comforter, Counselor) to Jesus' followers. Yet once more as in Acts, Jesus speaks of the relation of the Paraclete not only to his followers, but also of its relation to the world (vv. 8-11). The Paraclete will, by its presence among Jesus' followers (that is, within the Christian fellowship), be a witness against the disbelieving world (v. 9), which does not know that Jesus' worldly absence means his presence with the Father (v. 10) and which consequently, in the person of its ruler (i.e., Satan) stands under judgment for having rejected God because it has rejected the message of the Spirit-empowered church (v. 11).

In a sense, that message is even more convincing than the actual physical presence of Jesus, since it is only after his death and resurrection and the subsequent coming of the Spirit that one can understand the events of Jesus' life and their significance (v. 12; cf. 2:22; 13:7). Only in Spirit-informed remembrance of what Jesus did and said can such events and sayings be understood. That is the theological reality that shapes the canonical Gospels, and gives them their strange blend of history and interpretation.

That the Spirit can do that is due to the fact that its authority is that of God himself (v. 13; cf. Rom 8:27), as well as that of Jesus himself (v. 14). It is that unity of Father, Son, and Spirit that the church has in the presence of the Spirit.